Jonathan's Travels

By the same author

JONATHAN SWIFT: A LITERARY LIFE

JONATHAN SWIFT'S IRISH PAMPHLETS

JOHN BANVILLE: A CRITICAL STUDY

Jonathan's Travels
Swift and Ireland

❖

Joseph McMinn

Appletree Press/Belfast
St. Martin's Press/New York

*For my mother
and for Anna and Keavy*

First published by
The Appletree Press Ltd
19–21 Alfred Street
Belfast BT2 8DL
1994

Copyright © Joseph McMinn, 1994

All rights reserved. No part of this publication may be reproduced
or transmitted in any form or by any means, electronic or mechanical,
photocopying, recording or in any information or retrieval system,
without prior permission from the publisher.

A catalogue record for this
book is available from the British Library.
ISBN 0 86281 453 7

First published in the United States of America in 1994
by St. Martin's Press.
For information write:
Scholarly and Reference Division,
St. Martin's Press, 175 Fifth Avenue
New York, NY 10010
ISBN 0-312-12354-X
Library of Congress Cataloguing in Publication Data
McMinn, Joseph.
p.   cm.
Jonathan's Travels: Swift and Ireland / Joseph McMinn
Includes bibliographical references and index.
ISBN 0-312-12354-X
1. Swift, Jonathan, 1667–1745 – Knowledge – Ireland.
2. Swift, Jonathan, 1667–1745 – Journeys – Ireland.
3. Travelers – Ireland – History – 18th century.
4. Authors, Irish – 18th century – Biography.
5. Ireland – Civilization – 18th century. 6. Ireland – In literature.
7. Travel in literature. I. Title
PR3728.I67M36 1994
828'.509 – dc20 [B]
94-3781
CIP

TRAVAIL sb. ME. [O. Fr. *travail*, painful effort, trouble, work, f. *travailler*] 1. Bodily or mental labour or toil, especially of a painful or oppressive nature. 2. A work, a task; pl. labours. 3. The outcome of toil or labour; a (finished) 'work'; esp. a literary work. 4. The labour and pain of child-birth. 5. Journeying, a journey.

Oxford English Dictionary

Contents

	Foreword by Michael Foot	9
	Preface	11
	Introduction	15
1	Kilroot, County Antrim	21
2	Laracor, County Meath	32
3	Dublin and the Pale	51
4	A Tour of Munster	74
5	Quilca, County Cavan	89
6	The Irish Sea	105
7	Markethill, County Armagh	119
8	Final Journeys	133
	Epilogue	148
	Bibliography	151
	Index	157

Foreword

ALL THE world knows – or should know – how close was the association between Jonathan Swift and Ireland. He was born there, and died there. The imprint they left on each other is indelible. It may be still observed there today even by the casual traveller. The Dublin hospital to which he left his insignificant fortune opens new wards named after his women friends – yes, even Rebecca Dingley at last gets her due. The most recent seminar of Swiftian studies at Celbridge Abbey was opened by the President of Ireland, Mary Robinson. Sceptical financiers, expert or amateur, may see that, in the land which once rejected Wood's halfpence on his incitement, their £10 notes once carried the guarantee, the name and superscription of Jonathan Swift.

All the stranger, therefore, is it that no previous writer has sought to do what Joe McMinn does in this volume: to follow precisely in Swift's footsteps or, more usually, along his horse-tracks throughout the country. Apart even from his other interests, he was a great walker and an expert horseman, and these accomplishments and the fresh insights which they opened for him helped to achieve the reconciliation between him and the land of slaves to which he had been condemned.

Swift's own powers of invective – the supply seems inexhaustible – could be turned against his own countrymen and countrywomen. They can still scorch or consume their victims, as he intended. But he was no misanthrope, no hater of mankind or womankind, as Joe McMinn constantly insists and illustrates. He could turn his wit to almost any circumstance.

He was a master of raillery; indeed the word might have been invented just to suit him. He might have learnt or polished the gift in the London of Pope and Arbuthnot, Addison and Steele, but he learnt to give it a still lighter touch in the company of Patrick Delany and Thomas Sheridan, and all his captivated friends at Quilca and such like retreats. And this splendid company did not need to see any conflict between *Vive la Bagatelle* and his allegiance to the cause of "the whole people of Ireland".

Those friends included Esther Van Homrigh who lived at her ancestral home of Celbridge Abbey. Joe McMinn is much too honest an historian to exploit the connection he records, most affably, that Swift pictured Celbridge without "one Beech in all your Groves to carve a name upon", and how Vanessa might help her sister Molkin – "riding would do Molkin more good than any other thing provided fair days and warm cloaks be provided". He added, on the same theme, "I am getting an ill Head in this cursed Town, for want of Exercise. I wish I were to walk with you, fifty times about yr garden." How many times had he walked there and instructed her – to cite just one example – in the intimate revelations of Montaigne? Those beeches can be seen in those groves now.

Thanks to his journeys, with or without his correspondents in mind, Swift came to understand the real physical conditions in which the people of Ireland lived. He understood the famine of the late 1720s better than most observers, and resolved not to be just an observer. He might seem to take matters too flippantly: "Remove me from this land of slaves/Where all are fools, and all are knaves/And when their country lyse at stake/They only fight for fightings sake/While English sharpers take the pay/And then stand by to see fair play."

His travels amongst them helped to enlarge that Swiftian heart which hated human cruelty, as it had never been hated before.

Michael Foot

Preface

THE IDEA for this book was born out of a fascination with the footnotes to Swift's life in Ireland, observations and explanations by various editors and commentators on the daily routine of his social world, on the people and places he visited throughout his long and energetic career, and on the nature of the Irish landscape at the time. I began to sense the possibility of a story about his many journeys on the island, adventures which have a distinctive pattern largely shaped by his personality, and which help reveal the character and sensibility of the writer who produced one of the world's most fabulous tales of imaginative discovery, *Gulliver's Travels*.

Swift was a keen and committed observer of the country. His writings, most especially his letters, often tell us as much about early eighteenth-century Ireland as they do about himself. This study is not the first to discuss Swift's life in Ireland, but it is, I believe, the first to do so through the image of the traveller, through a series of topographical reflections. Anyone interested in his Irish career will find invaluable the major contributions of O. W. Ferguson's *Jonathan Swift and Ireland*, Carole Fabricant's *Swift's Landscape* and Irvin Ehrenpreis's biography, *Swift: The Man, His Works and The Age*, each of which, in its own way, has helped me to prepare my own version of that story.

My interest lies with significant and regular patterns of travel and friendship, with human landscapes which formed Swift's sense of Ireland. Swift was a resident citizen, not a detached visitor, and the many thousands of miles he spent riding around the country served his social, political and religious interests and concerns: places without people rarely moved him. This kind of attachment also explains why, unlike so many visitors and observers of the time, he never wrote a complacent line about Ireland. It also raises a significant distinction between Swift's pragmatic perspective on landscape and that of, say, the Romantic artist of the nineteenth century. Swift does not have a highly developed pictorial sense; neither is his literary humour the easiest to illustrate. A more general point about the relation between writing and landscape in early eighteenth-century Ireland deserves to be noted here. The golden age of Irish landscape-illustration postdates Swift's career, a fact related to the emergence of tourism, in the modern sense, at the end of the century. Where effective and appropriate, I have tried to include illustrations executed within Swift's lifetime, or as close to it as possible, but very often such efforts at authenticity have to give way to more suggestive work taken from a later period.

Researching this story has involved many journeys of my own, geographical and educational, following Swift's tracks and traces throughout Ireland, and learning from many people who helped complete my own efforts to recreate Swift's experience of the country. Virtually every corner of Ireland has something to recall about Swift, and I hope that this book does something to remind people of the Dean's enduring and imaginative role in Irish literature and history.

Over the past few years, many individuals, through conversation and correspondence, have helped me with my enquiries, and I warmly acknowledge assistance and encouragement from the following: Ronnie Bailie, Charles Benson, Mrs Guy Bloxam, Joe Brennan, Andrew Carpenter, Maurice Craig, Monica Curran, Michael DePorte, Paul Doherty, Richard Dutton, A. C. Elias, Olivia Fitzpatrick, Christopher Fox, Noel French, Brian

Graham, Brean Hammond, Alan Harrison, John De Courcy Ireland, Catherine Kelly, Br. Ronan Lennon O. H., Denis Loughran, Joe Lynch, Marie McFeeley, F. J. Mayes, Dáithí Ó hÓgáin, Hermann J. Real, Lona Roberts, Ian Campbell Ross, Br. Aloysius Shannon O. H., Mrs J. Troughton, Philip Wilson, David Woolley, James Woolley.

I owe a great deal to the library staff of the following institutions: Armagh County Museum; Armagh Public Library; The British Library; Carrickfergus Public Library; Cavan Public Library; Coolock Public Library, Dublin; Irish Architectural Archive; Irish Georgian Society; GPA Bolton Library, Cashel, Tipperary; Laois County Library; Linenhall Library, Belfast; Meath Heritage Centre; Merseyside Maritime Museum, Liverpool; National Gallery of Ireland; National Library of Ireland; National Library of Wales; Office of Public Works, Dublin; Orleans Public Gallery, Richmond, Surrey; Queen's University Belfast; Trinity College Dublin; Ulster Folk Museum; Ulster Museum; University of Ulster; Victoria and Albert Museum; Westmeath County Library; Williamson Art Gallery & Museum, Merseyside.

Professor Kevin Barry of University College Galway, and Dr Kevin Whelan of the Royal Irish Academy read an early draft-version of this study, and made many helpful observations and suggestions, for which I am very grateful. Any errors which remain are to be laid at my door. My brother Peter has helped me track down and understand some of the more exotic aspects of maritime history, and I thank him for his enthusiastic and helpful correspondence. My wife, Edna, has helped me throughout with proof-reading and critical advice: her unwavering faith has, as so often, encouraged and sustained my efforts.

In the search for suitable and effective illustrations for this study, I have enjoyed the advice and support of John Gamble, a gentleman and a scholar, who gave me generous time when it was needed, and from whom I have learnt a great deal. To himself and his good wife, Jean, who entertained me with patience and hospitality, a very special word of gratitude.

I am glad to acknowledge the financial assistance made available to me for completing this study from the British Academy and the Research Sub-Committee of the University of Ulster. I am especially grateful to Professor Robert Welch, who has consistently supported the enterprise. Janet Campbell, Jackie Darragh and Mary Williamson have done trojan work with typing, Paul Parkhill and Tony Feenan assisted me with the photography, Brian Graham and Kilian McDaid produced the special maps of Swift and Ireland, and I thank them all. My editor, Douglas Marshall, was always most helpful and patient with this work, which owes a great deal to his watchful attention.

Swift was never very kind about Wales, but he has been well served in this study by a most dedicated Welshman, Jonathan Williams, who persevered with the original idea, and saw it through to completion. To Jonathan, a final, and much deserved, thanks.

Permission from Gill and Macmillan to reproduce an extract from *The Hero in Irish Folk History* by Dáithí Ó hÓgáin is gratefully acknowledged. A short, exploratory version of this story was published in *Swift Studies* (1992), based on a lecture given at the Jonathan Swift Seminar at Celbridge Abbey, County Kildare, in 1991.

Introduction

THIS BOOK describes Swift's experience of Ireland. It attempts to document, illustrate and explain his various travels around the country, and to show how such travels entered into his imaginative sense of the island. The image of the adventurous voyager is central to Swift's most famous work, *Gulliver's Travels* (1726), a fantasy that reflects the author's fascination with remote but recognisable cultures. Born in Dublin in 1667, the son of English immigrants, Swift always retained a sense of curiosity and disbelief about the country of his birth, a land only a day's journey by boat from Britain, but one which sometimes seemed to him centuries apart in terms of civilisation.

Swift's detailed, perceptive, often critical, observations tell us a great deal about the landscape and culture of early eighteenth-century Ireland: they also give us an intimate understanding of his personal life and social world. Ireland may have seemed to him like a barbarous outpost, but he was no casual observer. Swift was a clergyman in the Church of Ireland for fifty years: the country was his home and his responsibility, a place to be explored, defended and, whenever possible, enjoyed. In his poetry, his pamphlets and, perhaps above all, in his correspondence, Swift reacted passionately to a country he regarded as at once familiar and strange, where the majority of the people did not even speak his language, but also a country

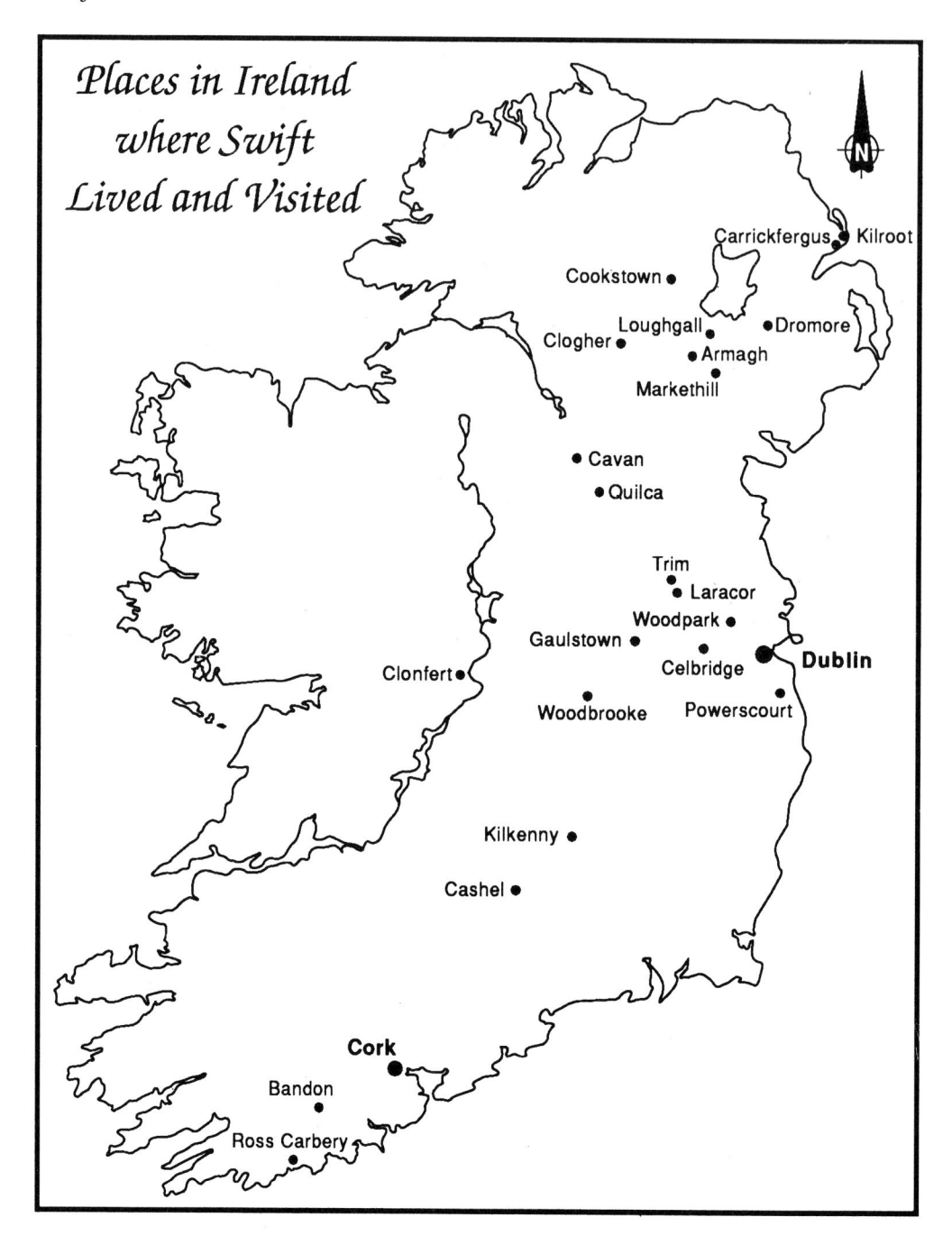

Places in Ireland where Swift Lived and Visited

which came to immortalise him as an "Hibernian Patriot".

Whenever Swift rode out from Dublin, he usually did so for reasons of friendship and health. His travels around Ireland were purposeful and practical, an invigorating way of keeping in regular touch with people who spent most of the year on their estates. Horse-riding, he firmly believed, was the ideal exercise; it kept illness at bay, ensured personal freedom of movement, and opened up the Irish countryside to the eyes of those who cared about its prosperity. Swift was never a tourist; rather, he was a man with a mission: landscape was there to be improved, not simply admired. Whenever he visited friends in the country, he always advised them to develop their land, often suggesting specific improvements. Swift saw the land as an economic resource and a political protectorate: Ireland was now entrusted to new owners, inspired by the biblical promise that the righteous would inherit the earth, whose task was to make a garden out of a wilderness, and thereby demonstrate their superiority to the Catholic natives.

Travellers in early eighteenth-century Ireland, whether they journeyed on horseback or by carriage, needed stamina and patience. Good roads were few and far between, and remained the private responsibility of local, county interests, usually those of wealthy landowners. A national system of turnpike-roads was proposed, and slowly introduced, in the 1730s, whereby users paid for the privilege of an improved highway, but the general quality of roads in Swift's lifetime was primitive and unpredictable, especially in winter. Travellers passed along roads which had hardly changed their surface or contours for hundreds of years, and moved through a largely unenclosed, underpopulated countryside which must have been extraordinarily quiet. The available maps of Ireland were helpful but often deceptive, never quite preparing the traveller for the shock and the demands of long journeys over bogland, highway and pass. During Swift's lifetime, the authoritative map of the island

To the best of my knowledge, the only surviving engraving of Swift the horseman. This appeared as the frontispiece to Essays Divine, Moral, and Political, *a satirical Whig pamphlet published in London in 1714. Using Swift's own tactic of ironical impersonation, the pamphlet seeks to expose him as a hypocritical time-server, a menace now back in Dublin where he belongs. The scene itself is of some enigmatic interest, with Swift setting off from the gates of his Deanery in pursuit of a post-boy and another (clerical?) rider, with his servant waving farewell. The pamphlet has been tentatively attributed to Thomas Burnet, an English lawyer. Artist unknown. (Courtesy of the Board of Trinity College Dublin)*

remained William Petty's *Hiberniae Delineatio* (1685), which saw many imitations but few real improvements until the latter decades of the eighteenth century.

Most of the country's population, variously estimated at

around three million, lived on the land, a subjugated peasantry whom Swift regarded with an alternating blend of pity and disgust. The ruins of the old Gaelic order were everywhere visible across the landscape, in the castles and the monasteries destroyed during the Cromwellian and Williamite wars of the seventeenth century. Many of Swift's journeys throughout Ireland were taken to visit fellow-clergymen – priests and bishops who enjoyed the distinction of belonging to the "Established Church", but who ministered to small, scattered congregations, often surrounded by an alienated populace. This clerical network within the Protestant settlement in Ireland forms a central pattern in Swift's expeditions around the country.

Swift's travels in Ireland usually took place during the summer months, when there was the best chance of reasonable weather and passable roads. He normally journeyed with servants (usually two of them, one riding in front, the other behind) whose job it was to protect their master, carry personal effects, secure suitable lodgings along the way, and tend to the welfare of the horses. Priding himself on his energy and determination, Swift liked to record the distance he could ride in a day, doing so in terms of the Irish mile, a thousand yards longer than the English measure of 1,760 yards. In his prime, he could average twenty-five miles a day; in his old age, still refusing the comfort of a carriage, he could manage only about fifteen miles a day.

Even statistically, the record of Swift's travels is impressive testimony to his energy, and a decisive clue to his understanding of contemporary Ireland. By the end of his life, he had passed through all four provinces, and most counties in the land. His sense of Ireland ranged from the new Scots-Presbyterian settlements along the east coast of Antrim to the largely uncharted and mountainous wilds of Kerry, from the stately demesnes of north County Dublin and Meath to the natural wonders of Fermanagh's Lough Erne. Swift's travels gave him the authority to speak out on Ireland's condition.

To follow Swift around the Ireland of his day gives us a vivid appreciation of his personality and his humour, makes a nonsense of the myth of a sour misanthrope, and restores something of the human and social character of his adventurous literary career.

1
Kilroot, County Antrim

SWIFT was born on 30 November 1667 in Hoey's Court, in the parish of St Werburgh, a district dominated by Dublin Castle and shaped by its mediaeval walls. Less than half a mile away, between St Bridget Street and St Patrick Street, stood St Patrick's Cathedral, on the south-western corner of the old city, at one end of the Coombe. Swift's parents were both from English families who had moved to Ireland earlier in the century in the hope of rapid advancement in a country enjoying relative peace after the Cromwellian wars. Swift's mother, Abigail Erick, was probably born in Dublin; his father, Jonathan, arrived with three brothers during the Restoration. All the brothers found employment within the expanding legal administration in the city, with Jonathan serving as steward to the King's Inns, the Law Society of Ireland. A daughter, Jane, was born to Jonathan and Abigail in 1666, but by the time their son was born, Swift's father had died.

One of Swift's uncles, Godwin, a successful lawyer and Attorney General for the Palatinate in Tipperary, stepped in immediately to support the widow Abigail, and ensured that the young Jonathan would enjoy some kind of paternal security. He also assumed educational responsibility for the boy, sending him to Kilkenny College at the age of six, while Abigail and her daughter returned to relatives in Leicester. Established on the Duke of Ormonde's estate, Kilkenny College was reputedly the best grammar school of its kind in Ireland, and Swift boarded here until he was fifteen. In 1682, he returned to Dublin and entered Trinity College, whose provost, Narcissus Marsh, would later establish his famous library in the shadow of St Patrick's Cathedral. An undistinguished scholar, Swift left Trinity College after seven years of undergraduate study with no clear idea about a career. Political instability must have intensified his personal sense of uncertainty: Ireland seemed to be preparing itself for war between the armies of King James II and William of Orange. Many of the staff and students at Trinity took the boat for England, where they felt safer, and from where they could observe the fate of the rebellion in Ireland. Swift joined the exodus, travelling across to stay with his mother in the city of Leicester.

After spending a few months with his mother, Swift travelled down to Oxford, where he applied for his MA at Hart Hall, and shortly thereafter obtained his first proper job, a post that was to have momentous implications for his literary career. He was appointed private secretary to Sir William Temple, a retired statesman and one of England's most distinguished and experienced diplomats. Temple's estate was at Moor Park, near Farnham in Surrey, where the twenty-one-year-old Swift arrived in the summer of 1689, and where he would remain, aside from two intervals of absence in Ireland, for the next ten years. On 5 November 1689, Temple was part of an official delegation that welcomed William of Orange on his landing at Torbay in England.

At Moor Park, Swift was introduced to a young girl called Esther Johnson, the eight-year-old daughter of one of Temple's housekeepers, and to Rebecca Dingley, a waiting-woman in the household. Esther Johnson would become Swift's closest, most inspirational friend in later years, celebrated by him as "Stella" in verse and prose. Both women would eventually follow him back to Ireland and would spend the rest of their days there.

"Swift and Stella", a fanciful representation of the young Swift tutoring the child Esther Johnson at Moor Park, by the English artist Margaret Isabel Dicksee (1858–1903). (With thanks to the Jonathan Swift Art Gallery, Kilroot)

After five years' service to Sir William Temple, Swift decided to enter the priesthood. When he returned to Dublin, in the spring of 1694, he found that the process of ordination would be both bureaucratic and slightly embarrassing. Narcissus Marsh, now Archbishop of Dublin, demanded that Swift obtain a detailed personal reference from Temple. Swift posted a dignified but nervous request to his former employer, apologising for the urgency of the reference, and explaining that since "above half the Clergy in this Town" were younger than him, he needed a respectable recommendation. At the age of twenty-six, Swift was being made to feel guilty for being so tardy about settling into a proper career. Temple complied with welcome alacrity. On 25 October 1694, Swift was ordained deacon; three months later, on 13 January 1695, he was ordained a priest by William Moreton, Bishop of Kildare, in Dublin's Christ Church Cathedral.

Swift did not have to wait long for his first appointment, but its location could hardly have been more disappointing. Lord Capel, one of the three Irish Lord Justices, directed the young clergyman to the prebend of Kilroot, just outside Carrickfergus in County Antrim. For Swift this must have seemed like a punishment rather than a preferment. His patent to Kilroot was dated 28 January 1695, and he arrived in this northern parish in March. On 28 April, he was officially installed in Lisburn, the cathedral town of the diocese of Connor, where he preached and read divine service.

The road from Dublin to Carrickfergus, about one hundred and ten miles, was the first of Swift's lengthy journeys in Ireland. It was also the first of many occasions in his life when he would head north on matters of business or friendship. Travelling along the coast road as far as Dundalk, he was still within the "Pale": he would have heard English as well as Irish spoken in the towns. After Newry lay the heartlands of the Glorious Revolution of 1690, Counties Down and Antrim, where Scottish Presbyterianism, rather than English Anglicanism, dominated the religious and political landscape. Passing through the small town of Belfast (home to a mere 2,000 inhabitants), Swift would have ridden up the shore-road which ran below the Cave Hill alongside the expanding waters of Belfast Lough.

Carrickfergus, which lay ten miles north of Belfast, was a fortified merchant-town, dominated by an impressive Norman castle which controlled all passage through Belfast Lough. It was here that William of Orange had landed on 14 June 1690 to complete his campaign against James II's forces. This part of the country was part of Swift's intellectual and religious inheritance, the birthplace of "Protestant liberty" and the theatre of its political mythology. The place would certainly have reminded him of one of his earliest literary compositions, "Ode to the King", written a few months after William's victory at the Battle of the Boyne (a river Swift would have crossed at Drogheda). This poem, com-

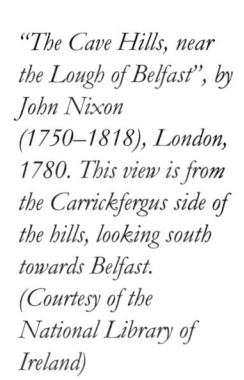

"The Cave Hills, near the Lough of Belfast", by John Nixon (1750–1818), London, 1780. This view is from the Carrickfergus side of the hills, looking south towards Belfast. (Courtesy of the National Library of Ireland)

posed in the classical form of a Pindaric Ode, pays solemn tribute to King William's heroic adventure:

> Thus has our prince completed every victory,
> And glad Iërne now may see
> Her sister isles are conquered too as well as she.

Although the poem was written five years before Swift came to live amongst Scottish Presbyterians, it already shows his inherited and inflexible hatred for Dissenters. According to the poem, one of William's greatest, almost incredible, achievements was his ability to control these fanatical sectaries:

> The Scots themselves, that discontented brood,
> Who always loudest for religion brawl,
> (As those do still wh' have none at all)
> Who claim so many titles to be Jews,
> (But, surely such whom God did never for his people choose)
> Still murmuring in their wilderness for food,
> Who pine us like a chronical disease;
> And one would think 'twere past omnipotence to please;
> Your presence all their native stubbornness controls,
> And for a while unbends their contradicting souls.

While Swift always accepted the necessity and justice of the Glorious Revolution, he never trusted the loyalties of Protestant Dissenters. Carrickfergus had heroic associations for Swift, but it had also been the gateway for the thousands of Scots immigrants who had settled, intractably, throughout Ulster. As far back as 1613, Rev. Edward Bryce had become the first Presbyterian minister to settle and preach in Ireland – in the prebend of Kilroot. In 1642, the first formal presbytery in Ireland was organised by Scots army regiments in Carrickfergus, soldiers sent over to quell the Irish rebellion. There was something ludicrous about Swift arriving in this area on behalf of the "Established Church": surveying the Antrim and Down coastlines, with Scotland clearly visible on a good day, Swift must have felt more like a missionary for a minority than a secure representative of the state church.

Kilroot itself (from the Irish *Cill Ruaidh*, "the red church", the site having a legendary association with a prehistorical battle) was an ancient Christian settlement founded in the late sixth century by St Colman. Up to the Reformation, it had been an important property of the Franciscan monks, who had built a church for the diocese on their land. When Swift arrived, the ruins of that monastic tradition were only picturesque monuments of the mediaeval Christian order. Swift's Anglican church could claim little advance on these emblems of decay and neglect.

The prebend of Kilroot must have struck Swift as something worse than a ghostly inheritance: there was no manse, no glebe, in Kilroot, not even a church. Tradition, rather than documentary evidence, suggests that he lived in a substantial cottage close to the shore of Belfast Lough. The prebend comprised three parishes: Kilroot, Templecorran and Ballynure. The only available church was in Ballynure village, a journey about ten miles to the west over the hills from the coast. A decade before Swift arrived in this most unpromising place, Richard Dobbs, a

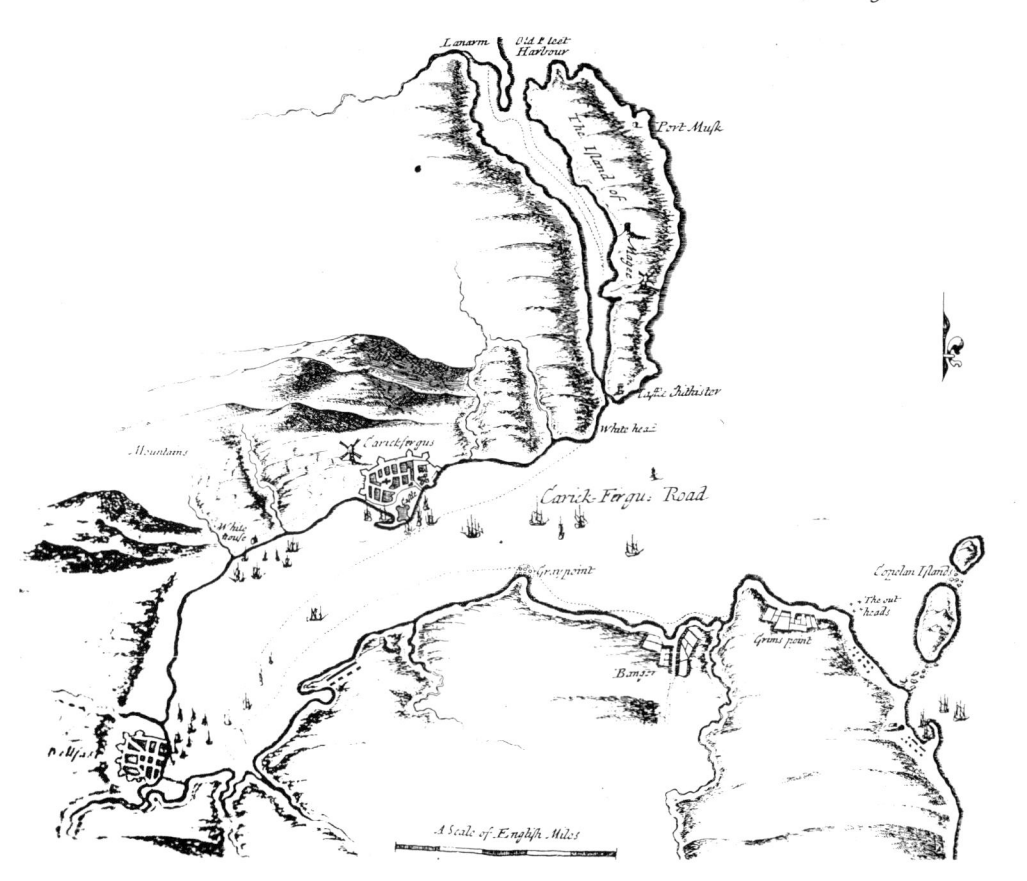

A military map of Belfast Lough from George Story's The Impartial History of the Wars of Ireland, *London, 1693. Story was a chaplain with the Williamite army.*

local squire and landlord, had written an extensive narrative on County Antrim, which contained the following observations:

> The parish of Kilroot is but small, the whole tithes not worth forty pounds, and the great tithes belong to the Earl of Donnegal, the small tithes to the Prebendary, one Milne, a Scotchman; the inhabitants (except my family and some half a dozen that live under me) all presbiterians and Scotch, not one natural Irish in the Parish, nor Papist; and may afford 100 men.

Dobbs had written his history of the county for William Molyneux of the Dublin Philosophical Society, and later became Lord Mayor of Carrickfergus. In June 1690, he welcomed King William to the town at the outset of the monarch's Irish campaign. Swift's potential congregation, we may infer, constituted a mere handful of local landowners and dignitaries who had subscribed to the Church of Ireland. In reality, however, the newly arrived clergyman made scant appearances at his occasional service in Ballynure. After the civilised and intimate security of Surrey, Swift must have been appalled at the monotony of this religious outpost.

Yet, despite his isolation, he did manage regular trips to Belfast, and even the odd one to Dublin. In Belfast he met Jane Waring, whom he nicknamed "Varina", the young daughter of a former Archdeacon of Dromore who had established the family home in Waringstown, about fifteen miles south-west of Belfast. Swift probably devoted more energy to this romantic liaison than to his clerical post, although both were to end in frustration. From a letter he wrote her in April 1696, shortly before he left Kilroot, we learn that Swift had determined on either marriage to Jane or, if that was refused, immediate return to Temple's household in Surrey. In a heavy-handed and imperious manner, he presented her with an ultimatum: marry him forthwith or never enjoy his company again. In this letter, the lowly cleric tries to seduce Jane Waring by adopting airs above his station, hinting at elevated social connections that he is prepared to sacrifice for her sake:

> I am once more offered the advantage to have the same acquaintance with greatness that I formerly enjoyed, and with better prospect of interest.

Jane, perhaps wisely, resisted Swift's combination of romantic appeal and insensitive threat. True to his word, he left Kilroot a couple of weeks after his overtures had failed, and turned back to Dublin to catch a boat for England. He arrived in Moor Park in May to resume his secretarial duties for Temple.

Swift had spent just over a year in Kilroot, yet he did not surrender his patent to the prebend for another eighteen months. In effect, he had abandoned his parish. Two years after his escape, he wrote to his successor, Rev. John Winder, to clear up some tithe accounts and bills. He also requested that the books he had left behind be properly packed and dispatched to him in Surrey. (Winder, rector of Carnmoney and a former friend of Swift from their time in Oxford, stayed on in Kilroot for twenty years.) On religious matters, Swift advised Winder to ignore those sermons he might come across, clearly uninterested in what he had once written for such an elusive congregation:

> Those sermons You have thought fitt to transcribe will utterly disgrace You, unless you have so much credit that whatever comes from You will pass; They were what I was firmly resolved to burn and especially some of them the idlest trifling stuff that ever was writt, calculated for a Church without a company or a roof; like our [Chapel at] Oxford.

That image of ruin and desolation, a mockery of the Church's temporal vitality, angered and offended Swift. His first clerical experience, of an anxious Anglican island surrounded by fundamentalist Dissent, would provoke his imaginative and literary ire for the rest of his life.

At the end of the letter to Winder, dated 1 April 1698, Swift asks him to pay an outstanding bill on his behalf to "Taylor of Loughbricland . . . for something about grazing a Horse and Farrier's bill". While Swift's memory for dates and places usually was shaky, his attention to financial detail was obsessive. Nine months later, in January 1699, he wrote again to Winder, and concluded with yet another inquiry about the settlement, this time referring to "Tailer the Innkeeper". Loughbrickland is on the main road between Belfast and Dublin, about thirty miles south of Carrickfergus. (It was in this area that William of Orange assembled his army before the Battle of the Boyne.) Details of this unpaid bill confirm that Swift did indeed ride the long road to Dublin during his time in Kilroot and, in this case, rested overnight in a safely Protestant town, while his horse was reshod and fed.

What may seem like a year wasted in Swift's clerical apprenticeship, a period outwardly marked by frustration and

Swift's cottage in Kilroot, "The Round House", from a photograph taken in the 1920s. (Courtesy of the Ulster Folk and Transport Museum)

disappointment, turns out to conceal a most extraordinary literary plot – the secretive composition of *A Tale of a Tub*, a scandalous satire on the theological lunacy and political danger of Dissent. Most commentators agree that the story was probably conceived during Swift's uneventful tenure at Kilroot. Surrounded by living examples of what he considered to be grotesque distortions of reasonable Protestantism, and having more than enough free time on his hands, Swift dreamed up this virtuoso piece of literary revenge. He never once mentioned it in his correspondence during this period, beginning a life-long literary strategy of personal concealment. There were also practical considerations behind this stylistic preference: publicising the fact that he was responsible for a satire on non-conformists might please his artistic vanity, but it might equally endanger a smooth path to a career in England, where toleration was more acceptable than in penal Ireland. (Swift clearly intended his *Tale* for an English audience and ensured that it was published in London, anonymously, in 1704.) When he arrived back in

Surrey, he was almost thirty years old, and still without a settled clerical career. Kilroot had certainly stimulated his artistic imagination, and shaped his sense of ironic attack and reserve, but it had not given him a greater sense of security.

The fundamentalist character of Kilroot has changed little since Swift's unhappy residence there, except that now the parish has a small, attractive church, St Colman's, built in 1971, and a regular congregation. At the back of the church sits a beautiful handmade model of "Dean Swift's Cottage", inspired by a photograph taken in the 1920s. The cottage itself was occupied until the 1950s, when it was destroyed by fire, and the remains buried in the foundations of a monstrous ICI chemical plant. Nearby stands the only sign of the writer's association with the place, the Jonathan Swift Art Gallery, which hosts regular exhibitions of modern Irish art, and which contains an interesting collection of Swiftiana.

Up in Ballynure, the remains of Swift's lonesome church are still visible, a small roofless shell in an overgrown graveyard, an image resonant of Swift's own characterisation of the place, as described to his successor three hundred years before.

2
Laracor, County Meath

AFTER his rather lonesome initiation into clerical life at Kilroot, Swift returned to his former employer, Sir William Temple, at Moor Park. He spent three more years there, fully occupied with arranging and editing his master's extensive correspondence and memoirs, and privately completing his own work on *A Tale of a Tub*. When Temple died in January 1699, Swift was left to settle the diplomat's literary legacy, while looking about for another employer to further his clerical ambition. Within a few months he was fortunate to be appointed domestic chaplain and private secretary to one of Ireland's Lord Justices, the Earl of Berkeley, who was staying in England. Swift was once again disappointed not to have found a permanent post in England, but he could count himself lucky to be in the household of an influential figure from the Irish administration. A valuable advantage of attending the Earl at Dublin Castle was the prospect of patronage through being close to the innermost workings of the Irish system of power and influence, and of being close to those who dispensed privilege and favour. Berkeley's legal and political responsibilities to the Crown also meant that Swift was obliged to accompany his master on many journeys between Dublin and London.

After a journey with Berkeley to Ireland in August 1699, Swift was granted the benefice of Laracor, County Meath. It comprised three parishes: the vicarage of Laracor, united with Agher and Rathbeggan. In many ways, this new post was a distinct improvement on Kilroot, since it enjoyed about £100 per annum through tithes (drawn from an area of over 4,000 acres) and was securely within the Pale – only twenty miles, less than a day's horse-ride, from the capital. Greater financial and cultural security had to be offset by the fact that Swift still represented a minority Church in a largely Catholic county, and that the vicarage had no manse and only a single-acre glebe. In 1682, just sixteen Protestant families were recorded in the area, but they were mostly wealthy landowners, most notably Garret Wesley, John Knightsbrook, both MPs for Meath, and Sir Arthur Langford, a baronet. The leading families of the parish had their own pews, and at the western end of the small church there was a turf-burning hearth. A small, but valuable, part of Swift's inheritance from the previous incumbent, Dr John Bolton (who had been appointed to the Deanery of Derry), was the prebendary of Dunlavin, County Wicklow, which ensured him additional annual tithes of twenty pounds. More significantly, it gave him right of attendance at St Patrick's Cathedral chapter, an important entry into the heart of the Church's administration.

Although Laracor still left many things to be desired, Swift developed a genuine affection for the place, deep in the Irish landscape of Meath, and worked hard at practical improvements for the vicarage. This was his first real home as a clergyman, and it remained part of his ecclesiastical estate until his death.

Over the next decade, Swift made the slow and unpredictable journey across the Irish Sea on seven occasions. Whether as Berkeley's chaplain, or as a delegate speaking on behalf of the Church of Ireland, the new vicar of Laracor always travelled as a servant of his employer's ambitions and designs. Privately, however, he was now beginning to shape his own literary identity. We know very little about his first few years as vicar, since no letters survive between July 1700 and August 1703, but this unusual silence must certainly cover his revision and completion of *A Tale of a Tub*.

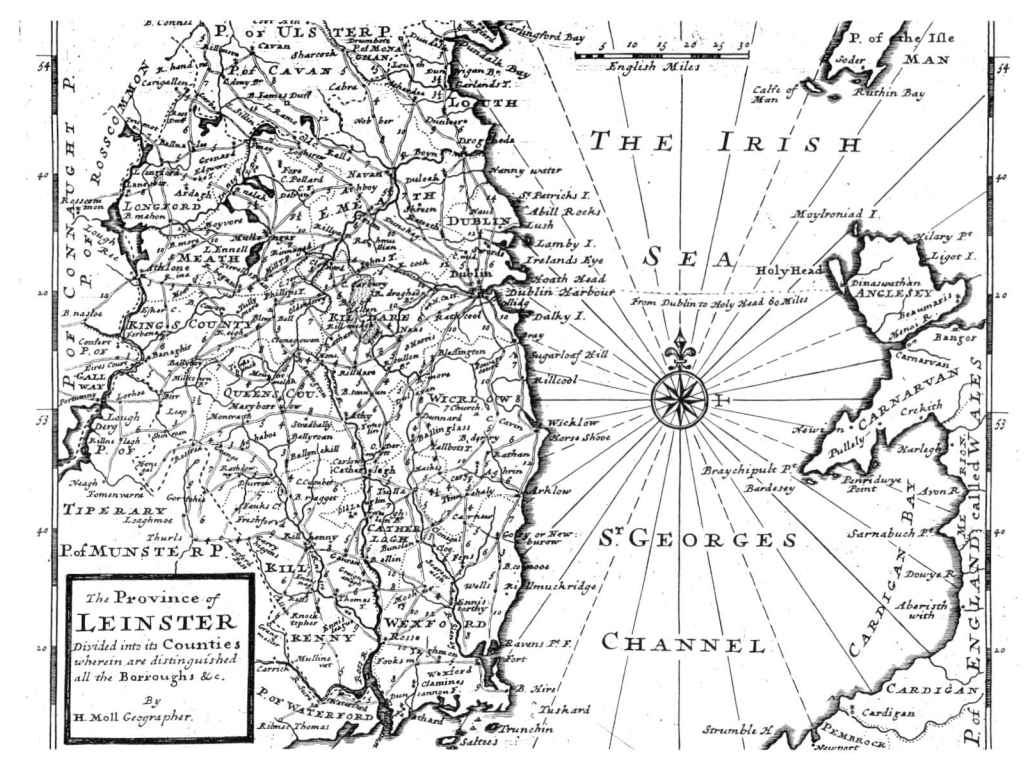

In November 1703, Swift left Dublin for London, where he delivered the manuscript of his *Tale* to a printer through the agency of a third party, hoping thereby to remain anonymous. The daring satire was published on 10 May 1704, and proved an immediate and notorious success. Three weeks later, Swift slipped back to Laracor. For a writer who nearly always concealed his true identity, who enjoyed his incendiary effects from afar, Ireland had considerable tactical advantages as an escape-route and a haven. It secured him literal, legal and artistic distance from the public reception of his work in England. A strong sense of caution, allied with a kind of inverted vanity, nearly always prompted Swift to remove himself from the

From A Set of Twenty New and Correct Maps of Ireland, *London, 1728, by the famous Dutch cartographer Hermann Moll, who never actually visited Ireland, choosing instead to produce improvements upon Petty's work. Two years before this set of maps appeared, Moll was ensured an unusual kind of literary immortality when some of his work was used to illustrate the first edition of* Gulliver's Travels.

immediate impact of his writings. Journeying regularly between England and Ireland, always looking at one country from the security of the other, writing for one audience but often on behalf of another, must have given Swift a most unusual, and exhilirating, sense of freedom about his literary identity.

Swift's ideological antipathy towards Dissent, intensified by his experience in County Antrim, dominated many of his writings in this period, even though the fixation found expression in a variety of forms. His personal convictions and beliefs, in so far as we can detect them, are rarely complex or surprising; his style and tone, however, because they nearly always involve an assumed identity, are usually shocking and volatile. His loathing for Dissent is matched by his rage over Ireland's subservience; both issues directed his attention to English interference in Ireland's internal affairs. Colonial radicalism of this kind, in which the mother country is forever scrutinised for signs of betrayal or neglect, in which the "English of Ireland", as Swift called them, feel they shoulder an unacknowledged political burden, is at the heart of his vexatious relationship with his ancestral home.

Swift was almost forty, and still vicar of Laracor, when he wrote his first pamphlet on Ireland. It was called *The Story of the Injured Lady*, an allegorical attack on England's imminent union with Scotland, and a defence of Ireland's moral and political demand for parity and justice. This allegory, written in early 1707, takes the personalised form of a lady's complaint to a friend about the dishonourable action of her former lover in choosing to marry another, scheming woman. The jilted victim describes the love-triangle in simple geographical terms:

> A Gentleman of the Neighbourhood had two Mistresses, another and myself; and he pretended honourable Love to us both. Our three Houses stood pretty near one another; his was parted from mine by a River, and from my Rival's by an old broken Wall.

In this melodramatic fable, venal England has betrayed a devoted and loyal Ireland in favour of a sluttish Scotland. In religious terms, this meant that Scottish Presbyterianism was being granted an honour denied to Irish Anglicanism. The Lady's sentimental appeal for justice cannot ignore the fact that the geographical link with Scotland, even if marked by an '"old broken Wall", seems less insurmountable than the distance from Ireland, coyly reduced to a mere "River". The Irish Sea seems a more truly "natural"' barrier, an image of real distance and separation, a physical measure of exile.

Swift tried hard to humanise Ireland's actual distress, even though the allegory forced attention towards the abstract political moral:

> ... one Third Part of my whole Income is spent on his Estate, and above another Third by his Tolls and Markets; and my poor Tenants are so sunk and impoverished, that, instead of maintaining me suitable to my Quality, they can hardly find me Cloaths to keep me warm, or provide the common Necessaries of Life for themselves.

Here begins Swift's lifelong preoccupation with Ireland's unnecessary and unnatural poverty. For someone as fastidious about personal economy as Swift, whose existence and authority depended on the fluctuating pattern of clerical tithes, money was the index of the country's normality and security. The year before he penned this tale, he had replied to an invitation from John Temple, a nephew of Sir William, to revisit Moor Park, and remarked on this unfortunate, but inescapable, bond: "If I love Ireland better than I did, it is because we are nearer related, for I am deeply allyed to its poverty." This is more than a mere conceit. Irish economic realities, especially those of famine, absenteeism and devaluation, shaped Swift's sense of justice, and provided him with an aggressive perspective on English rule. But he had to be circumspect as well as critical, sometimes foregoing the immediate satisfaction of seeing his work in print in favour of securing influential contacts. Indeed, he decided

"A Keith-Rigged Royal Yacht in a Breeze", by Johann van der Hagen (1675–1745). Painted c.1710, this shows the kind of armoured yacht used by the English government to ferry important people across the Irish Sea and the English channel. (Courtesy of the National Maritime Museum, Greenwich)

not to publish the *Story* (it was first printed in 1746, the year after his death) because it might antagonise those very Whigs with whom his Church had delegated him to negotiate.

At the end of 1707, Swift sailed to England to represent the Church of Ireland's case for the remission of the First Fruits, a traditional tax levied upon the Church by the Crown, specifically upon the income of clergymen like Swift himself. This tax had been suspended in England a few years earlier, by Queen Anne, and now Swift was in the difficult position of seeking a favour which he felt was a right. After waiting around the court for several months, he finally obtained an audience with Lord Godolphin, the Whig Treasurer, who tried to secure a quid pro quo from Swift, namely, an agreement to drop the Sacramental Test against Dissenters. Swift was indignant and uncompromising in his response, and soon composed a pseudonymous pamphlet in which he defended the political and pragmatic logic of penal legislation against Dissenters and Catholics. This time he was determined to publish, and *A Letter from a Member of the House of Commons in Ireland to a Member of the House of Commons in England Concerning the Sacramental Test* appeared in London in December 1708, a vigorous attack on the failure of English politicians to understand Anglican Ireland. From a modern liberal viewpoint, much of the pamphlet's case is an illogical defence of the indefensible, but it also shows some of Swift's best ironic touches when dealing with what he felt was unsolicited, self-seeking interest from England about uniquely Irish problems. The pamphlet also highlights his defence of the status quo in Ireland in terms of landed property. As the son of an English family, Swift sounds paradoxically contemptuous and distrustful of English designs upon his birthplace, always sensing that self-interest motivates English proposals for improvement:

> In short, whatever Advantage you propose to your selves by repealing the *Sacramental Test*, speak it out plainly, it is the best Argument you can use, for we value your Interest much more than our own. If your little Finger be sore, and you think a Poultice made of our *Vitals* will give it any Ease, speak the Word, and it shall be done.

Through this kind of mock-deference, Swift's fictional MP lectures his London colleague on the special political arrangement in Ireland, whereby the Anglican minority holds power: to extend or share that power, he points out, means simple self-destruction. He then provides a detailed account of Scottish settlers "in our *Northern Parts*", full of ironic praise for their industry, zeal and clannishness, emphasising their intolerance of English settlers and neighbours. As for the emotive and traditional appeal from England that all good Protestants should unite against their natural enemy, Popery, the MP substitutes fact for fiction, arguing that since Catholics are utterly dispossessed, there is no need to take them seriously:

> If we were under any real Fear of the *Papists* in this Kingdom, it would be hard to think us so stupid, as not to be equally apprehensive with *others*, since we are likely to be the greatest, and more immediate Sufferers; but, on the contrary, we look upon them to be altogether as inconsiderable as the Women and Children. Their Lands are almost entirely taken from them, and they are rendered uncapable of purchasing any more; and for the little that remains, Provision is made by the late Act against Popery, that it will daily crumble away. . . and, in the mean Time, the common People without Leaders, without Discipline, or natural Courage, being little better than *Hewers of Wood, and Drawers of Water*, are out of all Capacity of doing any Mischief, if they were ever so well inclined.

The logic employed by Swift's persona is brutal but incontestable. Survival in colonial Ireland, only twenty years after the Williamite settlement, depends on ownership of the land and the absolute right to its wealth. This is the first time in Swift's writings on Ireland that we get a picture evoking what Daniel Corkery later called "The Hidden Ireland", the shattered world of the Gaelic order, a majority without power of any kind, whose poets continued to dream of the return of Bonnie Prince Charlie and the restoration of their ancestral homes.

Swift always felt surrounded by an alien culture, whether it was the Scots of Antrim, or the Catholic peasantry outside the Pale. In early eighteenth-century Ireland, the Anglican population had to consolidate its position in the country and, in particular, to rectify and protect the impoverished state of its temporalities. This kind of national context helps us to understand Swift's individual passion for "improvement", a contemporary term whose dilettantish connotations might, misleadingly, suggest a leisurely indulgence of amateur taste. The truth of the situation, however, lay revealed in decaying manses, parishes without parishoners, declining income from tithes: in short, a Church as impoverished as the state it claimed to represent.

Trim Castle, in County Meath, by Paul Sandby, London, 1778. Sandby, the leading English watercolourist, was sent many drawings by Irish artists, and later included them in his Virtuosi's Museum *(1781), a collection of scenes taken from all over the British Isles. (Courtesy of the National Library of Ireland)*

In the first ten years of his vicarage at Laracor, Swift was often absent from his parish, and delegated responsibility to his curate, Thomas Warburton. Nearly half this period was spent by him in London, an absence which, it could be argued, diminished the force of his regular attacks on non-resident clergy. Responsibility had to be balanced with ambition, however, and Swift worked hard at both. The historical record of his vicarage shows that, whenever resident, he devoted himself energetically to its material improvement, asserted his clerical authority over his new parish, and enjoyed the social company of his small community.

Laracor could not offer its vicar a proper home, so Swift generally resided in Trim, the principal town of the diocese of Meath, described by Swift's biographer, Irving Ehrenpreis, as "a busy and important Protestant island in a sea of Roman

Catholicism". Trim had been a strategic town of the English Pale for centuries, an ecclesiastical centre and military outpost straddling the River Boyne. It was dominated by the massive walls of Hugh de Lacy's Anglo-Norman castle, the site of a decisive battle in 1649, when Cromwellian forces had besieged and captured the town, retaking it from the Catholic Confederation. The rector of Trim, John Stearne (later to become Swift's predecessor as Dean of St Patrick's), naturally became a close acquaintance of the new vicar. Two months after taking up the vicarage, but still living in Dublin, Swift wrote a long letter to his first love, Jane Waring, in which he acknowledged the continuing dilemma of being practically homeless:

> . . . the place of residence for that they have given me is within a mile of a town called *Trim*, twenty miles from hence; and there is no other way but to hire a house at *Trim*, or build one on the spot: the first is hardly to be done, and the other I am too poor to perform at present.

Once he arrived in Laracor, he began to landscape his solitary glebe and took great proprietorial satisfaction in cultivating the appearance of the place. He spent several pounds on planting a garden of cherry, holly and apple trees, arranging rows of willows along the bank of the Knightsbrook River and laying out a path alongside it. (The name of the place derives from the Irish, "Lathrach Cora", meaning "the site of the weir".) He spent £10 on repairing the church's chancel, and began to supervise the building of a small cottage on the glebe as a temporary home for the vicarage. The quality of this transformation was officially recognised in 1723 when, in a Church of Ireland report into the state of ecclesiastical properties in the county, the glebe was described as "exceedingly well-inclosed", with "a neat cabin made by the present incumbent", and valued at £60. The small church itself was also praised for being properly ceiled and flagged. Such details about Swift's industry ought not to be read as a quaint footnote to the more serious business of his literary career; his love of order, his practical concern for the welfare of his Church and, most significantly, his understanding of virtuous citizenship as active public service, are as much in evidence in the domestic routine of his everyday business as in the literary fictions of his satirical imagination.

Swift employed two local men in the running of his property, Isaiah Parsivol as tithe-agent and steward, and Joe Beaumont, a linen merchant in Trim, as financial adviser and factotum. Dr Anthony Raymond succeeded Stearne as rector of Trim in 1703, and became a close friend of Swift. (Raymond, unlike Swift, was keenly interested in the Gaelic tradition, learned Irish and accomplished significant antiquarian research, meeting regularly with Gaelic scholars and poets in and around Dublin.) Church affairs were in the hands of Swift and his curate, but also extended to the parish clerk, Roger Cox, about whom an amusing anecdote is told by Lord Orrery, later to become one of Swift's friends and one of his first biographers. It seems that Swift's parishioners did not always attend his services and that he once arrived with his faithful clerk to face an empty church. After a decent delay, Swift, determined to persevere, declaimed, "Dearly beloved Roger, the Scripture moveth you and me in sundry places." Such incidents, if true, must have summoned up bad dreams of Kilroot.

The tone of references to his parish in Swift's correspondence varies from weary resignation to playful intimacy. In January 1709, he wrote to Archbishop King of Dublin, saying he felt "wholely useless in *Ireland*, and in a Parish with an Audience of half a Score", but in April the following year, writing to Dean Stearne, he sounds happily immersed in the routines of country life:

> I am here quarrelling with the frosty weather, for spoiling my poor half dozen of Blossoms. Spes anni collapsa ruit, whether those words be mine or Virgils, I cannot determine . . . I am this minute very busy, being to preach to day before an Audience of at least 15 People, most of them Gentle, and all Simple.

> I can send you no News; only the Employment of my Parishoners may for memory sake be reduced under these Heads, Mr Percivall is ditching, Mrs Percivall in her Kitchin, Mr Wesley switching, Mrs Wesley stiching, Sr Arthur Langford, riching, which is a new word for heaping up Riches; I know no other Rhime but Bitching, and that I hope we are all past.

There is no doubt that Swift enjoyed his rustic role in a parish where he could count on some educated society as well as feel relatively independent within a quiet ministry. After the disappointments of Kilroot, Swift was beginning to discover a more congenial Ireland, in a more stable part of the country, which could accommodate his religious authority and in which he could exercise his natural sociability.

Some of Swift's most pleasurable company in these early years at Laracor was no doubt with the young ladies, Esther Johnson and Rebecca Dingley, who had been persuaded to follow him and settle in Dublin after Temple's death. They had both arrived in 1701, when Johnson was twenty-years old. When they were invited to Laracor, they usually stayed with Dr Raymond in Trim: Raymond's friendliness towards the young English ladies endeared him to Swift. On other occasions, the ladies stayed in a cottage beside Knightsbrook Gate, on the Percivall estate, a residence that came to be known locally as "Stella's Cottage" (it was inhabited up to the 1960s). When such company arrived in Trim, Swift arranged social evenings for several of his parishioners and friends. These sessions were dominated by backgammon and card games, especially piquet, basset and ombre. Cards were always played for money, with Swift later entering his wins or losses carefully into his account-book. Sometimes the social ritual was transferred to Dublin, where Dean Stearne and even Archbishop King occasionally joined the party.

For Swift, travels in Ireland were nearly always undertaken in the interests of friendship. Although his circle at Laracor offered a cosy intimacy, he made a point of maintaining contact with old friends, not all of whom lived at a convenient distance.

Within Meath, he often called at Wood Park, the estate of Charles Ford, a young friend who remained loyal to Swift throughout his life, finally helping him assemble his literary legacy in his old age. Swift frequently called upon the Ashe brothers at their family home in Finglas, on the northern outskirts of Dublin. Dillon Ashe was the vicar of Finglas, and St George Ashe, who had been Swift's tutor at Trinity College, was Bishop of Clogher. In November 1709, Swift bought himself a new horse and set off to visit St George Ashe in the cathedral town of Clogher, County Tyrone, a journey of about eighty miles. He stayed with the Ashe family for four weeks, during which time he records winning sixteen shillings at cards. On his way home, he visited Thomas Parnell, Archdeacon of Clogher, a young poet who was later to join Swift in the Scriblerus Society of Pope and Gay in London. That Christmas was spent by Swift in Laracor, where he continued to plant willows and to clear the land for the spring.

Rural contentment did not result in a particularly rich literary harvest. Establishing and consolidating his new vicarage, while developing new patterns of friendship within and beyond Laracor, seem to have satisfied most of Swift's energies during these years. He had written a few pamphlets on Irish affairs, not so much for the benefit of his countrymen, more to censure English politicians. The playful side of his literary personality is heard in one of several poems he wrote while vicar of Laracor, entitled "On the Little House by the Churchyard at Castleknock". This whimsical narrative tells of a vicarage just outside the northern limits of Dublin, on the Navan road, which had been almost levelled by a storm, and is now a vivid image of clerical misery:

> The vicar once a week creeps in,
> Sits with his knees up to his chin;
> Here cons his notes, and takes a whet,
> Till a small ragged flock is met.

An unusual, somewhat crude, engraving of Stella, based on an original drawing by Rev. Thomas Parnell, possibly done in 1716. In 1768 it was included as the frontispiece to Vol.XVII of Swift's Works *by the Dublin printer George Faulkner, who owned the drawing, since lost. (Courtesy of the National Library of Ireland)*

As the story develops, most of Swift's Laracor friends pass by, each one trying, without success, to guess what the ruin used to be: Esther Johnson suggests an illicit still, Dr Raymond a "pigmy's tomb", Warburton a pigeon house. The company agrees to restore the site, with Swift to supply "willow sticks" from his glebe, and Joe Beaumont to donate the bricks. This kind of informal verse was usually composed for pure entertainment, circulated amongst friends and rarely considered for serious publication.

The sociable and leisurely years at Laracor were drawing to a close, however, when Swift set off for London in August 1710, to renew his previous efforts at remission of the First Fruits. The Whig government was in crisis, and it seemed as if the Tories, were they to form a new administration, might be more sympathetic. After ten years at Laracor, Swift was now moving towards the very heart of English politics, where he would enjoy three years of valuable patronage and extraordinary influence.

On his journey down to London, Swift stopped overnight at Chester, where he began a very special correspondence with Esther Johnson, which continued for the next three years. Sixty-five letters survived from this intimate diary, posthumously arranged and edited as his *Journal to Stella*. Historians and literary critics have viewed the correspondence as a vivid account of Swift's life in London, especially as an eye-witness record of the Tory administration led by Bolingbroke and Harley. Because it was written for a close friend who had been left behind, the *Journal* repeatedly evokes images of the simpler, more "natural" life at Laracor. As propagandist for the Tories, Swift is keen to impress Esther with his new authority and social circles, but also tries to suggest a moral distinction between a necessary service in England and a more contented residence in Ireland. The provincial vicar was now a confidant of the ruling-class in Britain, clearly thriving on the challenge and opportunity, but he did not want Stella to feel that she and Ireland were forgotten. Sometimes he explained his continued absence by pleading powerlessness: "I long to be in Ireland; but the ministry beg me to stay." It is difficult to take his professed exasperation seriously, since he had always dreamed of escape from the Irish backwater to some – almost any – English appointment. And yet his nostalgia for a more independent, less fraught, way of life becomes a lyrical motif in the *Journal*:

> ... yet I would fain be at the Beginning of my Willows growing. Percivll tells me that the Quicksetts upon the flatt in the Garden, do not grow so well as those famous ones on the Ditch. They want digging about them; the Cherry trees by the River side my heart is sett upon.

Laracor came to represent a form of pastoral, of certainty and stability, especially when imagined from the unpredictable metropolitan world of government and intrigue. Too ironic by temperament to become an earnest devotee of the pastoral Muse, Swift could nevertheless sense the corruptive influence of writing for political masters:

> See how my Stile is altered by living & thinking & talking among these People, instead of my Canal & river walk, and Willows.

After three years of living what he called "the life of a Spider", Swift was too closely identified with the Tory party to escape the general political crisis of 1713, when it became clear that the Whigs, whom he had pilloried and mocked, would soon return to power. In the spring of that year, he was informed that he would be granted the Deanery of St Patrick's and not, as he had hoped, a bishopric in England. Swift came home to Dublin in June, sick and dejected and, after making arrangements for his transfer to the Deanery, retired to the peace of Laracor to reflect upon what he considered to be an humiliating reward for three years' dedicated service.

A few weeks after his return, Swift wrote a letter to an attractive young woman in London, Esther Van Homrigh, whom he had met during his three years there, and with whom he had established a discreet romance. He had acknowledged this acquaintance to Esther Johnson, but not its intimacy. In the letter, Swift sounds like, or plays the part of, a hermit resigned to his country retreat, having experienced the folly and vanity of civilised life abroad:

> I design to pass the greatest part of the time I stay in Ireland here in the Cabin where I am now writing, neither will I leave the Kingdom till I am sent for, and if they have no further service for me, I will never see England again: At my first coming I thought I should have dyed with Discontent, and was horribly melancholy while they were installing me, but it begins to wear off, and change to Dullness. My River walk is extremely pretty, and my Canal in great Beauty, and I see Trout playing in it.

Swift's pastoral haven also provides him with a conceit which contrasts productive with thankless labour:

> ... I am now fitter to look after Willows, and to cutt Hedges than meddle with Affairs of State. I must order one of the Workmen to drive those Cows out of my Island, and make up the Ditch again; a Work much more proper for a Country Vicar than driving out Factions and fencing against them.

Knowing that Swift's greatest literary triumphs, in both Ireland and England, are yet to come, and that he would serve the Deanery of St Patrick's with commitment and passion for the rest of his life, it is amusing to hear such talk of stoical withdrawal. Swift could never have been content with such a permanent self-exile from the public domain, especially not in Ireland. Laracor may have become a pleasant and comforting dream, but after his experience in London, it intensified his suspicion of English politics, and served as a personal model of sanity and order.

Financial as well as emotional attachments to Laracor ensured that Swift retained his control over the vicarage even after his move to Dublin. At the end of his *Journal*, he had told Stella, "I shall not part with Laracor: that is all I have to live on." Life at the Deanery would certainly be more expensive, and the parsimonious Swift wanted to retain, and if possible increase, his original tithes. To complete his long-standing

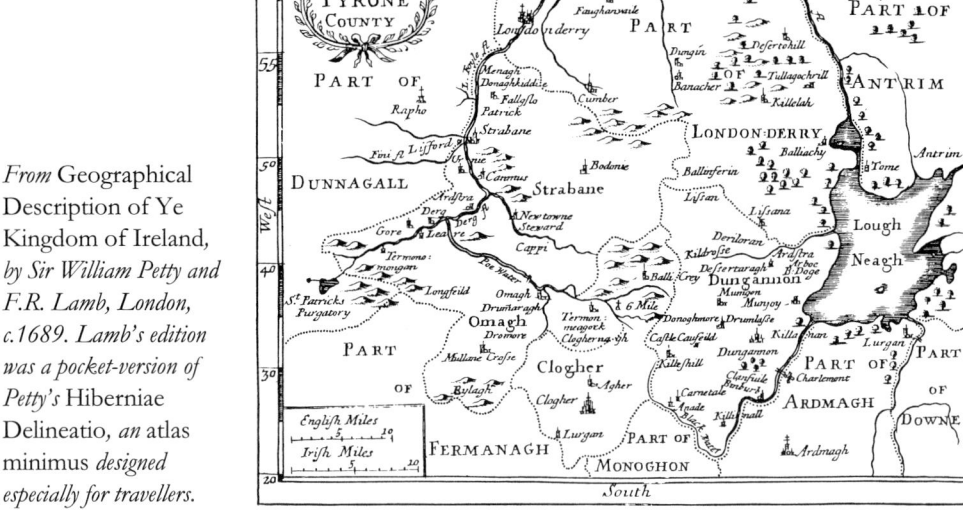

From Geographical Description of Ye Kingdom of Ireland, *by Sir William Petty and F.R. Lamb, London, c.1689. Lamb's edition was a pocket-version of Petty's* Hiberniae Delineatio, *an atlas minimus designed especially for travellers.*

determination to enrich the incumbency, particularly the glebe, in 1716 he started negotiations with John Percival, who owned land adjoining the humble Laracor acre. After what he called "a hundred delays", Swift secured an additional twenty acres for the glebe. This cost him £200, paid to Percival by the Church of Ireland's Trustees for the First Fruits, the remission of which Swift himself had finally helped to secure. A further, more modest, addition to the vicarage was the impropriate tithes of Effernock, a small rectory in the neighbouring parish of Trim, tithes which had earlier passed from clerical to secular ownership.

An impressive example of practising what he preached, Swift had transformed Laracor from a homeless, impoverished cure to a domesticated vicarage with valuable landed-property. In his will, drawn up in 1742, he bequeathed the tithes of the parish to the vicars of Laracor, but only on the condition that "the present Episcopal Religion shall continue to be the National Established Faith and Profession in this Kingdom". In the

Swift's chapel at Laracor today.

event of the disestablishment of the Church of Ireland, he asked for the tithes of the parish to be distributed to the local poor. His bequest, and his anticipation of what he considered would be a religious disaster, reveal both his uncompromising loyalty and his genuine charity.

Swift's little church at the crossroads of Laracor survived until 1857, when it was rebuilt and refurbished. It continued to serve a declining parish until 1979, when it was sold. No longer a church-property, it still stands, once again renovated and re-roofed, and is now a picturesque family home.

3

Dublin and the Pale

WHEN SWIFT first entered the Deanery House of his new cathedral, the city of Dublin was slowly beginning to shed its mediaeval character, but it had yet to display those monuments and symbols which eventually distinguished it as a Georgian metropolis, second only to London in its grandeur. In the early years of the eighteenth century, the population was about 60,000 people, about the same as present-day Galway or Derry. Having been the centre of colonial power for so long, Dublin was largely Protestant and English-speaking, although increasing numbers of Catholics were beginning to move into the city, resulting in a doubling of the city's population during Swift's lifetime.

Nearly all the great public buildings in Dublin, such as Trinity College and the two great cathedrals, St Patrick's and Christ Church were on the more densely populated south side of the River Liffey. One of the first, and possibly the most elegant, of these urban landmarks was the Royal Hospital at Kilmainham, begun in 1680 by William Robinson, Surveyor General, which lay to the west of the city, close to the river. One of Robinson's last contributions to the expanding capital was Marsh's Library, begun in 1703, beside St Patrick's. The next Surveyor General, Thomas Burgh, made a major impact on the city's architecture in the first decade of the century, designing a new Custom House in Essex Street (replaced by another one, on the north

A PROSPECT of the CITY of DUBLIN from the NORTH

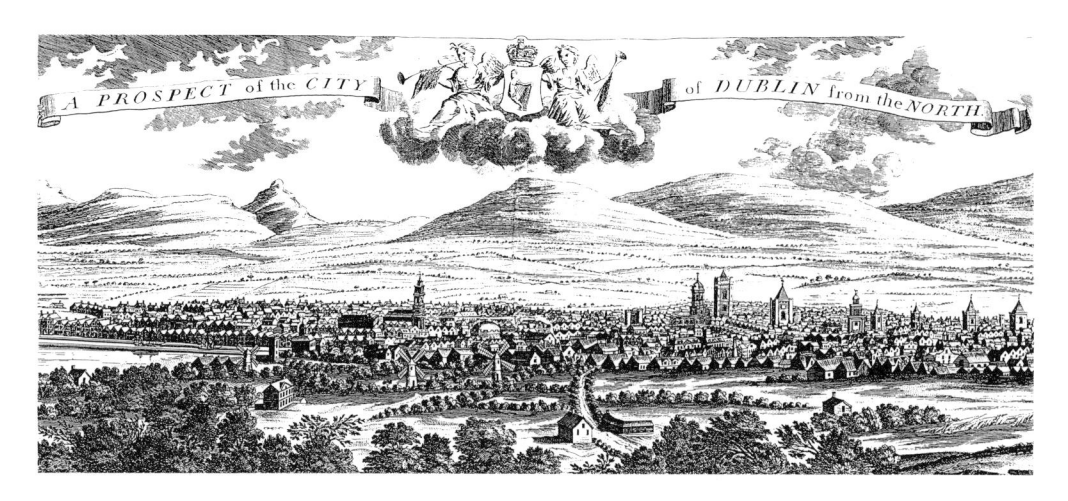

side of the river, at the end of the century). Burgh also began the building of a new library for Trinity College, a project which continued for two decades. Also on the north side of the river, beside Oxmantown Green, Burgh set out the imposing new Royal Barracks (later Collins Barracks). Beyond this vast military complex, further up the river, stood Parkgate, entrance to the most extensive park in these islands, Phoenix Park, one of the great public legacies of the Duke of Ormonde when he served as Viceroy in the latter half of the seventeenth century. The municipal headquarters of the city was the Tholsel, built in 1676, situated in Skinner's Row, just behind Christ Church. In 1715, Joshua Dawson sold Dublin Corporation a new house for the Lord Mayor, one he had built for himself ten years previously on the north side of St Stephen's Green in the street which bears his name.

Swift had little evidence of Dublin's Georgian splendours in domestic architecture, since so many of these signs of a new prosperity and confidence appeared late in his lifetime. The systematic town-planning of fashionable streets and squares, associated with such wealthy families as Dawson, Leeson, Molesworth and Gardiner, only began to assume definitive and lasting shape during the 1730s, when residential developments

From Charles Brooking's Map of the City and Suburbs of Dublin, *Dublin, 1728, the standard and most popular map of the capital in Swift's lifetime.*

THE ROYAL HOSPITAL

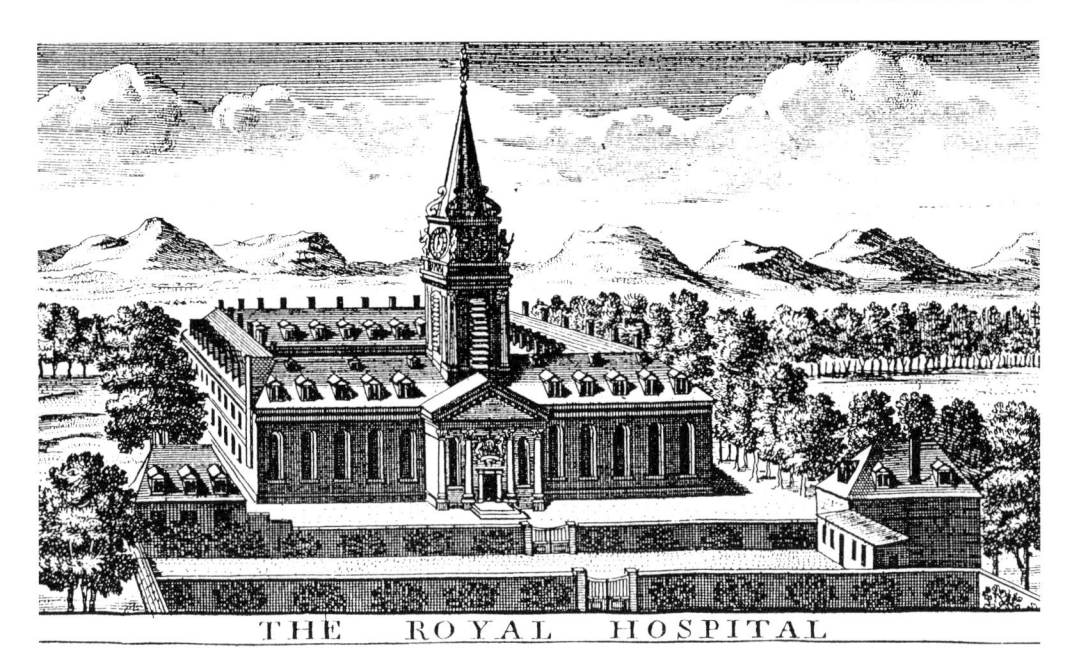

From Brooking's Map of the City and Suburbs of Dublin *(1728)*

on the north and south-western sides of the city transformed the aesthetic character of the capital. Crossing to the north of the city at Essex Bridge, the first of Dublin's five bridges spanning the Liffey, one entered directly into Capel Street, the long residential artery which divided the parishes of St Mary's and St Michan's. Many of Swift's friends and acquaintances had established their town-houses in this increasingly affluent area, conveniently situated in relation to the city's affairs, but at a healthy distance from its mediaeval alleyways. The golden age of townhouses for the nobility coincides almost too neatly with Swift's decline. In 1745, the year of Swift's death, Richard Cassel's Leinster House, built for the Earls of Kildare (now the Dáil, seat of the Irish parliament), set a new standard of elegance for the south side of the city.

One of the most spectacular mansions built during Swift's time as Dean of St Patrick's was Castletown House, in Celbridge, County Kildare, twelve miles west of the city.

Designed for the most part by Edward Lovett Pearce, and built in 1722, this majestic residence was the home of William Conolly, Speaker of the Irish House of Commons, reputedly one of the wealthiest men in Ireland. Conolly, the son of a Donegal innkeeper, was one of Ireland's *nouveaux riches*. Castletown remains the most dramatic Palladian mansion in Ireland. Also in Celbridge, in grounds through which the Liffey begins its final flow towards the city, stood Celbridge Abbey, the ancestral home of Esther Van Homrigh.

In August 1714, sensing that she was planning to return to Celbridge in order to be close to him, Swift wrote to Esther, warning her about the parochialism of Ireland:

> It is not a Place for any Freedom, but where every thing is known in a Week, and magnifyed a hundred Degrees.

Reluctant as ever to identify with Ireland, as if his background was always ready to disgrace or embarrass him in polite company, he urged his all-too-passionate friend to exercise social and political decorum. If she chose to settle in Ireland, a prospect that both flattered and unnerved him, he advised her to prepare for the shock. Ironically, it was Swift who was in for a surprise, when Esther suddenly appeared in Dublin in the autumn, and took lodgings in Turnstile Alley, beside the Parliament buildings. Shortly before he had left London to take up his new post, Swift had tried to forestall such a move, and to distance himself imaginatively, in the longest poem he was ever to write, *Cadenus and Vanessa*, in which he had pleaded middle-age responsibilities as the reason for his inability to return her passion. Vanessa, however, was determined to pursue her clerical lover.

With both Stella and Vanessa now in the same city, the new Dean of St Patrick's assumed his ecclesiastical duties and began to explore Dublin's social world. He was now one of the most important clerical figures in the city, whose rank introduced him into the

Castletown House, Celbridge, County Kildare. (Courtesy of the Irish Architectural Archive)

higher reaches of Irish society. In his early years at the Deanery, Swift abandoned Dublin in favour of the country at the least excuse, partly because he believed regular horse-riding was good for his health, but also because so many of his friends, old and new, lived for most of the year in the countryside, coming up to Dublin only for ceremonial occasions, such as the rare appearance of the Lord Lieutenant and the opening of Parliament. Swift's seasonal departure for the country followed a general exodus, since most well-to-do people left Dublin during the summer, escaping from its noise, dirt and congestion. There was also his continuing interest in, and obligation to, Laracor. He conducted a great deal of his business from Trim rather than Dublin, often delegating responsibility for Deanery affairs to his deacon. Residence at Trim, in the heart of County Meath, meant that he was only a day's ride from most of the country estates he liked to visit.

The first of these rural expeditions was undertaken by Swift only two months after his return from England. He set out to visit a friend, Knightley Chetwode, whose Woodbrooke estate lay just outside Portarlington, County Laois, then called Queen's

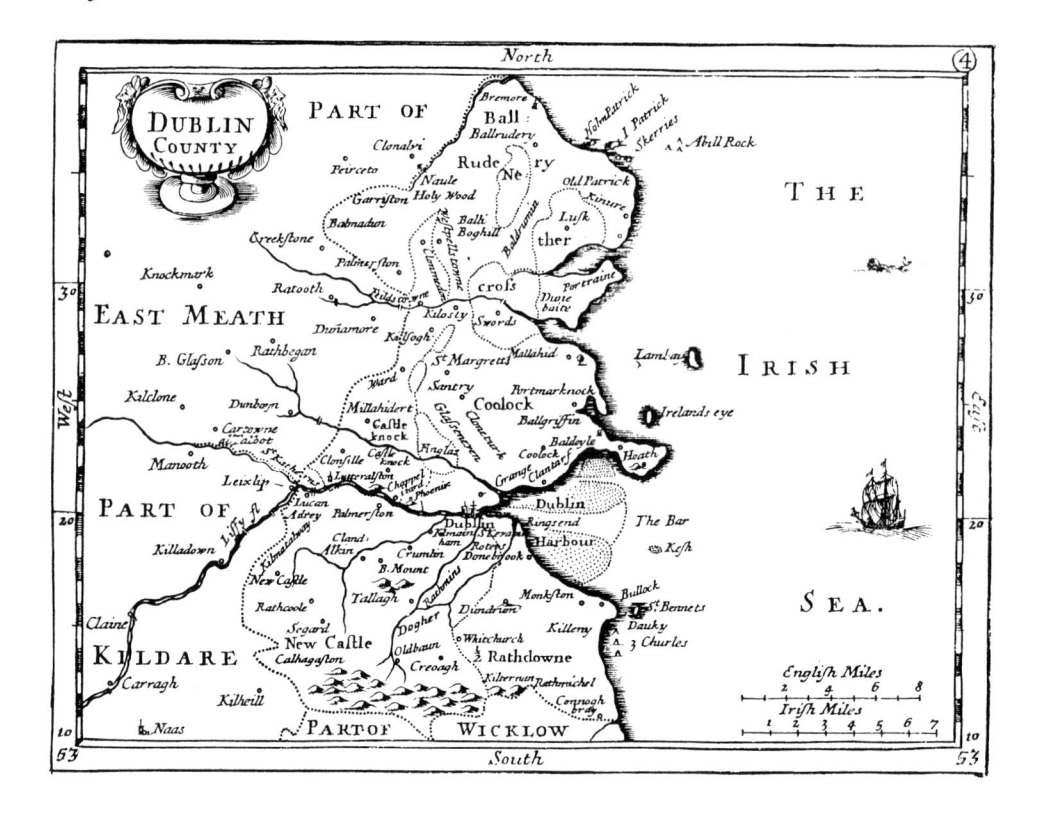

County. Chetwode was a wealthy young landowner descended from English gentry who had settled in Ireland in the previous century. Besides Woodbrooke, he owned a second country residence at Martry, County Meath, just outside Navan, about twelve miles north of Laracor. Flattered to be receiving the renowned Dean, Chetwode offered to send a coach to bring his guest from Trim to the estate, to which Swift replied breezily, "I scorn your coach; for I find upon trial I can ride." Three years in London had left Swift out of practice, but he was now determined to commence a new regimen for himself.

Only a short while after setting out, Swift encountered one of Vanessa's servants, who tried, unsuccessfully, to deliver a message to the impatient Dean. Swift rode on south to Phillipstown (now called Daingean), about twenty-five miles

From Geographical Description of Ye Kingdom of Ireland, *Petty and Lamb, c.1689.*

from Trim, where he rested, and then wrote a message to Vanessa:

> I met yr Servant when I was a mile from Trim, and could send him no other Answer than I did; for I was going abroad by Appointment; besides I would not have gone to Kildrohod [i. e. Celbridge] to see you for all the World. I ever told you, you wanted Discretion. I am going to a Friend upon a Promise, and shall stay with him about a fortnight: and then come to Town, and I will call on you as soon as I can.

Clearly nervous about Vanessa's proximity, and relieved to have an excuse to travel on, Swift arrived at Woodbrooke only to find the Chetwodes gone out to a christening feast in the neighbourhood. They soon returned, however, with Swift glad that the day's "tedious Journy", about thirty-five miles riding, was over.

As was to become his custom, Swift overstayed his invitation, and enjoyed his winter break for almost a month. He described his stay with Chetwode to Archdeacon Thomas Walls, a friend in Dublin, beginning, as usual, with his health:

> I am used very well, and ride out whenever the weather will let me, and have been in tolerable Health, though realy I think I used more Exercise in Dublin, for in this Country of Ireld there is no walking in Winter.

He tells Walls that he has visited several towns in the area, "all better than Trim", although he does not name them. Always on the watch for signs of potential improvement and development, Swift remarks on the abundance of local "Wood and Hedges", and imagines the place in summer would be "a sort of England onely for the Bogs". Situated at the southern tip of the vast Bog of Allen, Chetwode's estate was viewed by Swift as a model of English order, but one surrounded by very unEnglish features, which accentuated its effect. Domesticating the landscape was a form of practical industry which Swift saw as both virtuous and necessary. He complimented his host on his "employments of improving bogs", and could not resist doing some gardening and landscaping of his own at Woodbrooke on a site Chetwode later referred to as "the Dean's field". In the summer following this visit, Chetwode wrote to Swift, pleased to report on the fruition of his visitor's labours:

> The Dean's field flourishes, the quicks are cleared and grow well; it is a fine thing to have a good lawn, they talk of mowing it, I assure you. Your river walk is thirty feet wide, has in all its windings and meanders, as we suppose, about five thousand foot in length.

Few occupations gave Swift greater satisfaction than this kind of practical husbandry, a personal form of healthy industry he had first cultivated in his vicarage at Laracor.

While staying at Woodbrooke, Swift attended to some clerical business in the area by visiting lands that belonged to St Patrick's in the parish of Kilberry, north of the town of Athy, in neighbouring County Kildare, about ten miles south-east of Chetwode's estate. In a letter to Chetwode, written after this visit, Swift detailed the financial income of this ecclesiastical property, comprised of "1700 and odd acres", and listed the townlands of "Bert, Cloney, Arowland, Kilcolman, Oldcourt, and Tullygorey, Prusselstown, Shanraheen, Tyrellstown, Clonwarrir, and Russelstown", remarking irritably upon "those cursed Irish names". He lamented the fact that the young forests in the area had been "horribly abused", presumably cut for fuel instead of being allowed to grow for a variety of uses.

Even though Swift instinctively complained about Ireland, and regularly made a point of contrasting its barbarity with the beauty of England, it is clear that he soon enjoyed the hospitality and company of a number of the landed gentry. Some of these figures, such as Peter Ludlow of Ardsallagh, near Navan, were occasional friends who would always welcome a visit from Swift; others, like Charles Ford, whose estate lay halfway between Trim and Dublin, became life-long friends. The Anglo-Irish gentry of the fertile pasturelands of Meath and Kildare were a society within a society, a wealthy ruling-class consolidating its presence in Ireland through industry, cultivation and the building of great country houses.

Knightley Chetwode helped introduce Swift to many new friendships within this colonial network, one of the most enduring being that with the Rochfort family of Gaulstown, at Rochfortbridge, County Westmeath, about forty miles due west of Dublin on the Galway road. Robert Rochfort, the head of this distinguished family, had been Attorney General for Ireland, and later Speaker of the Irish House of Commons. In 1707, he became Chief Baron of the Irish Exchequer. Like Swift, he was a principled Tory, a loyalty which led to his removal from office in 1714 when the Whigs returned to power. Such mistreatment of a public servant by the government would have endeared him to the Dean.

Swift became particularly friendly with two of the sons, George and John "Nim" Rochfort, both of whom were Irish MPs. George took over the country estate in 1704 on his marriage to Lady Betty Moore, daughter of the Earl of Drogheda. Their eldest son, Robert, later became the first Earl of Belvedere. His marriage to the sixteen-year-old daughter of Lord Molesworth, in 1736, became a local sensation when, after suspecting a romantic affair between his brother Arthur and his young bride, he imprisoned her in their new family home, Gaulstown House, for nearly thirty years. In 1740, the embittered husband employed Richard Castle to build Belvedere Villa on the shores of Lough Ennell, to which he retired. In the grounds of the Villa, he built the "Jealous Wall", the largest sham-ruin in Ireland, to prevent him seeing the neighbouring house of the hated brother. The house at Rochfortbridge in which Swift originally stayed was burnt down in 1920 and later was demolished.

Swift first visited Gaulstown in May 1715, in the company of Chetwode, and returned regularly over the next few years. His longest, and most celebrated, visit was in the summer of 1721 when he stayed with the Rochforts from June to October. On that occasion, he was part of a large social gathering of new friends and acquaintances which included three clergymen, Thomas Sheridan, schoolteacher and scholar, Patrick Delany, Fellow of Trinity College, one of Swift's earliest biographers, and Dan Jackson, vicar of Santry and occasional comic-versifier. Shortly after he arrived at Gaulstown, Swift wrote to Vanessa, complaining of his "weary Journy in an Irish Stage Coach". (The Dublin-Kinnegad public-coach was one of the first of its kind in Ireland, and had begun only in 1718.) That Swift should have travelled by public transport was most unusual for such a determined horseman, but he explained the drastic change of habit by the temporary absence of a reliable and spirited horse of his own. Never a very relaxed, or relaxing, visitor, he goes on to tell Vanessa that he is "as deep employed in othr Folks Plantations and Ditchings as if they were my own Concern", obviously mindful of how his horticultural zeal might disconcert his hosts.

A view of Lough Ennell, with Belvedere Villa and Gaulstown House in the background, from Jonathan Fisher's Scenery of Ireland, London, 1795.

From letters written to other friends while holidaying in Gaulstown, we learn that Swift spent a great deal of time in vigorous exercise, riding around the area and rowing on the artificial lakes on the estate. On one occasion, his energy exceeded his caution and he was tipped into the lake, getting a heavy soaking. Blustery, rainy weather prevented him from several rambles on horseback which he had intended, including one to Athlone, nearly thirty miles west of Gaulstown. Charles Jervas, who had painted Swift's portrait in both London and Dublin, visited his own property in neighbouring Offaly, then called King's County, although a vexed Swift discovered this only after Jervas had returned to London. In a letter to his Archbishop, William King, Swift sang the praises of rural therapy, declared the good sense of occasional indulgence in trivial pastimes, and repeated the motto of his leisure-time in London, *vive la bagatelle*.

By early October 1721, however, Swift sensed that the summer visit was over, and returned to Dublin. Realising that he had left some personal articles behind him (including a silver sweet-box) he wrote to Dan Jackson asking for their return. In this same letter, he confides his suspicion of having overstayed his welcome:

> I talk upon a supposition, that Mr Rochfort had a mind to keep me longer, which I will allow in him and you, but not one of the family besides, who I confess had reason enough to be weary of a man, who entered into none of their tastes, nor pleasures, nor fancies, nor opinions, nor talk.

But he then goes on to express satisfaction at having completed such an expedition:

> I baited at Cloncurry, and got to Leixlip between three and four, saw the curiosities there, and the next morning came to Dublin by eight o'clock, and was at prayers in my cathedral. There's a traveller.

Aged fifty-three, Swift feels a special kind of triumph in testing himself against such journeys, and enjoys defying those bouts of dizziness and nausea which so often afflicted him, and which are now understood to have been caused by Ménière's syndrome, a chronic disorder of the inner ear.

Two very different literary compositions resulted from Swift's stay at Gaulstown and confirm his desire to celebrate the friendship which such visits encouraged. The first was a poem, "The Part of a Summer", a comic pastoral about the characters and company at Gaulstown. Written in lively rhyming couplets, it is an indulgent series of character sketches, including one of Swift himself as spartan taskmaster:

> At seven, the Dean in night-gown dressed,
> Goes round the house to wake the rest:
> At nine, grave Nim and George facetious,
> Go to the Dean to read Lucretius.

Swift makes the most of the irony whereby the besieged hosts cannot escape from their guest: he could always see the demanding side of his social personality, and regularly subjected himself to this kind of poetical rebuke. The other literary composition sponsored by this summer was an essay of instruction for a young bride, *A Letter to a Very Young Lady, on her Marriage*. This formal epistle was written for the marriage between John Rochfort and Deborah Staunton, which took place in January 1723. Both bride and groom were good friends of the Dean.

It must have struck Vanessa as a cruel irony that the man whom she had followed to Ireland could spend so much time and energy travelling around the country in search of convivial company, while she waited, with less and less patience, for a stealthy visit from her lover. In one of his first letters addressed to her at Turnstile Alley, Swift enquired about her health, and posed rhetorical questions about her country home in County Kildare:

> Does not Dublin look very dirty to You, and the country very miserable. Is Kildrohod as beautifull as Windsr [*sic*], and as agreeable to you as the Prebends Lodgings there; is there any walk about you as pleasant as the Avenue, and the Marlborough Lodge.

Vanessa, by Philip Hussey (1713–1783). (Courtesy of the National Gallery of Ireland)

The implied understanding, of course, was that, after the royal grandeur of places like Windsor, Irish villages such as Celbridge seemed unworthy of their inhabitants, part of a hopeless comparison in standards of civility and taste. Rural Ireland could never hope to compete with the English standard, although it would always be rendered by Swift with greater interest and conviction.

In the summer of 1720, Vanessa decided to move out of Dublin and settle at the Abbey in Celbridge, mostly for the sake of her consumptive sister Mary, nicknamed "Molkin" by Swift.

Celbridge Abbey, County Kildare. Vanessa's ancestral home was redesigned at the end of the eighteenth century, and is an outstanding example of Georgian Gothic. One of the most important contemporary links with Swift's legacy, it is now the home of the St John of God Brothers, who have transformed the grounds as part of their project for the help of the mentally and physically handicapped. (With thanks to Celbridge Abbey)

In the six years she had spent in Ireland, Vanessa had never once enjoyed Swift's company at the Abbey, a place he declined to visit on his own for fear of scandal. In August, he wrote to Vanessa and declared that he and his friend Charles Ford would shortly be paying her a visit. In the course of the letter, Swift playfully pictures the grounds at Celbridge, without "one Beech in all your Groves to carve a name on, nor a purling Stream for love or money, except a great River, which sometimes roars, but never murmurs".

We know nothing about Swift's first visit to Celbridge, but from a letter he wrote in October we can easily guess that it included the usual compulsory recreation. He told Vanessa that "riding would do Molkin more good than any other Thing, provided fair days and warm Cloaths be provided", and added, on the same theme, "I am getting an ill Head in this cursed Toun for want of Exercise. I wish I were to walk with you fifty times about yr Garden." Celbridge was an imaginary haven which Swift rarely dared visit. He had told Vanessa that he "ever feared the Tattle of this nasty Toun", and was mindful that they often shared the same society.

As Dean of St Patrick's, Swift soon found himself in the company of most of the influential families around Dublin. Several of his friends lived on the fashionable northside of the city: Patrick Delany in Glasnevin, the brothers John and Dan Jackson in Finglas and Santry, and the Grattans at Belcamp, in Raheny. Most of these friendships were based on clerical ties: Rev Patrick Grattan, for example, had held a prebend in St Patrick's. When Swift began his visits to Belcamp in late 1714, one of Grattan's seven sons, Robert, had taken over the father's prebend. (Henry, the eldest son, was the grandfather of the patriot figure of the last decades of the century. The Grattan home at Belcamp was inhabited until the 1970s, when it was abandoned, and then vandalised. Just down the road, however, John Jackson's beautiful Georgian villa, "Woodlands", built around 1730, still stands resplendent.)

Swift spent his first Christmas as Dean with the Grattans at Belcamp. In a letter to Thomas Walls, shortly after his arrival, he described to his hosts the farcical manner of his journey. We learn that he chose to go by ferry from the city to the northside, and instructed his two servants, Will and Tom, to take the horses along the coast road and to await the arrival of the boat. When the Dean disembarked, he found both men hopelessly drunk. The "two Loobyes", as he calls them, were incapable of even helping their master put on his riding-coat. A furious Swift eventually mounted his horse, named "Bolingbroke", and was soon followed by Tom, "drunk as a dog" and careering all over the strand behind his master. Swift finally managed to subdue him, and dismissed the hapless servant on the spot, only to realise later that Tom had gone off with his "Quill & Brush for my Teeth". Swift viewed his servants' duties very seriously, but the reality of an existence dependent on reliable servants was more often a comedy of manners than a display of decorum.

In his first few years as Dean, most of Swift's excursions to visit friends in the countryside were a relatively short ride from either Dublin or Trim, distances that usually could be covered in a day. Only once during these early years did he undertake a major journey outside the Pale. This was a trip made in the spring of 1717, with John Stearne, to Clogher in County Tyrone, the cathedral town he had last visited eight years previously when vicar of Laracor. Stearne was riding north for his enthronment as the new Bishop of Clogher and had asked Swift to accompany him. The two clergymen set off together from Drogheda, travelled north along the coast road to Newry, and then turned inland towards the city of Armagh, the ecclesiastical capital of Ireland. Clogher lay about twenty-five miles west of Armagh, midway between Dungannon and Enniskillen.

After three days at Clogher, they headed for Stearne's old episcopal house at Magheralin in County Down, only thirteen miles south of Belfast. They stayed there for three weeks, most of Stearne's time being spent on clearing out his old residence, making it ready for the incoming bishop, Ralph Lambert, formerly Dean of Down. Swift, so meticulous in his own domestic arrangements, was amused to see that Stearne was missing so many of his household items, including "Candlesticks, by the dozen, and Bottles by the Hundred". Whenever he toured the immediate area, certain places would have had a strong nostalgic association for Swift. Lisburn, where he had been formally installed as a priest of the diocese twenty-two years before, lay only four miles to the north, and Waringstown, ancestral home of Jane Waring, was within walking-distance, less than two miles to the south.

Stearne's business completed, he and Swift left Magheralin on 20 May, and travelled south on the main road to Dublin as far as Drogheda, where they parted ways. Stearne rode on to the capital, but Swift headed inland to Navan, where he stayed overnight, finishing the last few miles to Trim the following

Belcamp, Raheny, County Dublin. One of the last residents of Belcamp was the Irish feminist and republican, Constance Markievicz, who rented the house and grounds in 1909, when she set up a communal training-camp for na Fianna, the Republican youth-movement. Photograph taken by George Farran, a former owner of Belcamp, in June 1898. (With thanks to Mrs Guy Bloxam and Coolock Public Library)

morning. When he arrived in Trim, he was sorry to learn that his former rector, and friend, from Laracor, Thomas Warburton, had passed through on the previous day on his way north to Magherafelt.

Only a few weeks after returning from Magheralin, Swift wrote from Dublin to an old friend, Robert Cope MP, of Loughgall, County Armagh, "I could with great satisfaction pass a month or two among you, if things would permit." Swift had certainly visited Cope during his stay at Magheralin (Loughgall lay about thirty miles away) and now recalls, "I stayed three weeks at Trim after I left you, out of perfect hatred to this place, where at length business dragged me against my will." In fact, on this occasion Swift was unable to return to Cope, and spent the month of August with Peter Ludlow at Ardsallagh, eight miles north of Trim. It is easy to forget that Dublin was Swift's actual home during this period, since he rarely stayed for very long in the Deanery. Even during the long winter months at the Deanery, when weather usually prevented spontaneous trips abroad, Swift would dream of the joys and benefits of escape, as in the following verses, "The Author's Manner of Living", composed at the end of 1718:

> On rainy days alone I dine,
> Upon a chick, and pint of wine.
> On rainy days, I dine alone,
> And pick my chicken to the bone:
> But this my servants much enrages,
> No scraps remain to save board-wages.
> In weather fine I nothing spend,
> But often sponge upon a friend:
> Yet where he's not so rich as I;
> I pay my club, and so God b'y' –

There is a seasonal as well as a daily economy at work here: for such a spartan, but just, economist, the depressions of a Dublin winter were as much financial as emotional. Summers with wealthy hosts were cheaper than the Deanery with dependent servants.

Swift's decisive preference for the countryside was based on a life-long obsession with its beneficial influence on his health: the joys and disappointments of travel were, accordingly, bound up with the same fixation. In the spring of 1719, he cancelled a proposed visit to Aix-la-Chapelle in France, blaming the ill-health of his supposed travelling companion, Samuel Dopping, MP for Trinity College and a son of the Bishop of Meath. Dopping was "not thought strong enough by his Physicians to undertake so long a Journey", according to Swift, who, in a letter to Charles Ford, promised to console himself with "a more lazy Remedy of Irish Country Air". A puritanical streak in his personality was always on the look-out for signs of idleness, and he constantly nagged himself and others about the necessity and benefit of physical exercise, preferably horse-riding. In May 1719, he wrote to Ford:

> I am absolutely ordered to ride, and my Health having grown somewhat better, I have bought a Horse at a great Price, and am resolved to ramble about this Scurvy Country this Summer, and take the Shame to my self of being lazy and irresolute.

The best-known, certainly the most popular, portrait of Swift, painted by Charles Jervas about 1718, when the Dean was aged fifty. (Courtesy of the National Portrait Gallery, London)

The emotional relation between health and mobility could become a torture for Swift, since travel, the supposed remedy for illness, often proved impossible because of illness. To journey around Ireland required a high degree of physical fitness and mental determination: a sick man could be maddened by the knowledge that the cure might kill him. In April 1720, at the end of a year dominated by bouts of sickness which marooned him in Dublin, he wrote again to Ford:

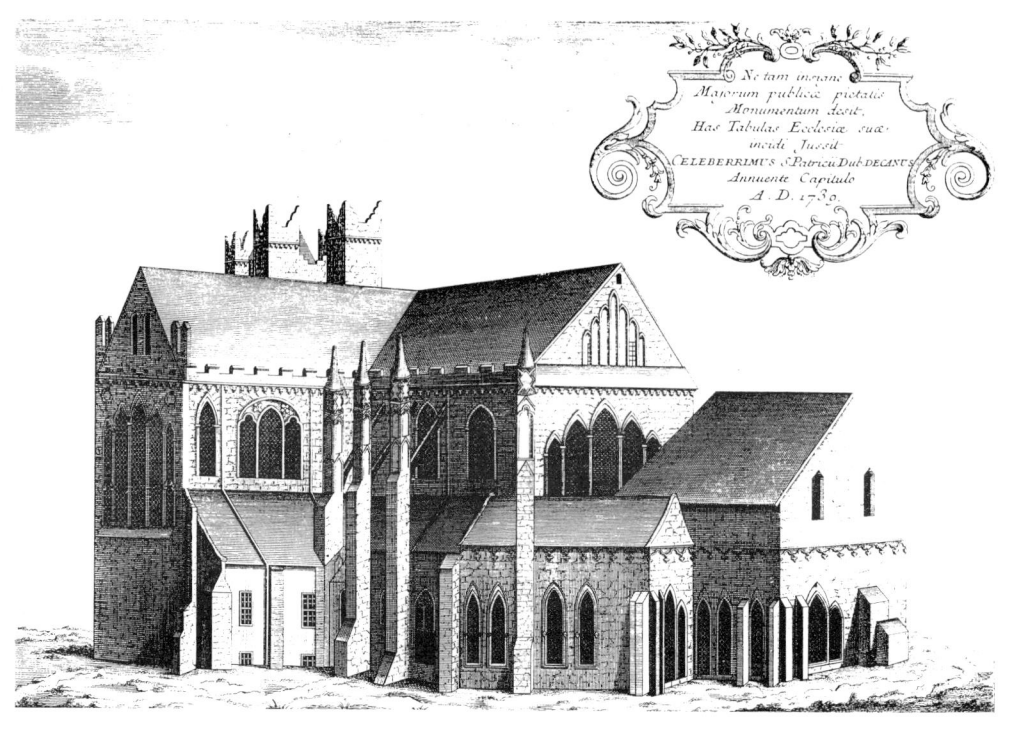

I am hardly a Month free from a Deafness which continues another month on me, and dejects me so, that I can not bear the thoughts of stirring out, or suffering any one to see me, and this is the most mortal Impediment to all Thoughts of travelling, and I should dy with Spleen to be in such a Condition in strange Places; so that I must wait till I grow better, or sink under it if I am worse. You healthy People cannot judge of the sickly.

In his sick-bed, or simply confined to the Deanery, Swift could only imagine those travels which were forbidden to him. The ability and the freedom to travel were a kind of emotional (because physical) triumph of his energetic and restless personality.

The literary dimension of that personality soon began to absorb a new sense of the Irish landscape and its people. Swift developed a sharper sense of observation, which expressed itself through graphic imagery and an intimate, informed style. In 1720, this new receptiveness to the Irish scene produced a lively and memorable poem, "The Description of an Irish

An architectural engraving of St Patrick's cathedral, from The Works of Sir James Ware Concerning Ireland, *translated and revised by Walter Harris, Vol. I, Dublin, 1739. This shows clearly the outline of the cathedral familiar to Swift, a decade before the granite spire erected by George Semple onto the Minot tower, an addition Swift never lived to see.*

Feast", a version of a Gaelic poem, "Pléaráca na Ruarcach", attributed to the Leitrim poet Hugh Mac Gauran. The facts of this poetic interchange between Gaelic poet and Anglican Dean are elusive, but it seems that Swift heard a rendition of the poem, asked for a prose translation, and then composed his own, shorter version. Swift gives us, in effect, a "native" version of *vive la bagatelle*:

> They dance in a round,
> Cutting capers and ramping,
> A mercy the ground
> Did not burst with their stamping,
> The floor is all wet
> With leaps and with jumps,
> While the water and sweat,
> Splishsplash in their pumps.
> Bless you late and early
> Laughlin O'Enagin,
> By my hand you dance rarely,
> Margery Grinagin.
> Bring straw for our bed,
> Shake it down to the feet,
> Then over us spread,
> The winnowing sheet.
> To show, I don't flinch,
> Fill the bowl up again,
> Then give us a pinch
> Of your sneezing, a Yean.

Legend has it that the famous Gaelic poet and harpist Turlough Ó Carolan (1670–1738) played his own version of the "Pléaráca" for Swift and Patrick Delany at the Deanery. The story is remarkable because exceptional: Swift's attitude to Gaelic culture was generally contemptuous.

As far as the Protestants of Ireland were concerned, however, Swift soon emerged from his deceptive retirement and became rhetorical champion of their cause. In May 1720, seven years after moving back to Dublin, he published his first polemical pamphlet on Irish affairs. Entitled *A Proposal for the Universal Use of Irish Manufacture*, the pamphlet attacked English mercantilist legislation which penalised Irish exports and, in retaliation, urged a boycott of English imports. The anonymous speaker, confident of his audience's understanding, quotes outrageous remarks in deliberately casual fashion:

> I heard the late Archbishop of Tuam mention a pleasant Observation of some Body's; "that Ireland would never be happy 'till a law were made for burning everything that came from England except their people and their coals.'"

Swift was also enraged by the rapacity and ignorance of Irish landlords, a class with which he was very familiar. A new kind of outraged sympathy now enters the appeal:

> Whoever travels this Country, and observes the Face of nature or the Faces, and Habits, and Dwellings of the Natives, will hardly think himself in a Land where either Law, Religion, or common Humanity is professed.

The speaker declares that the misery of the Irish peasantry, whom he has observed, is greater than that of "the peasants in France, or the vassals in Germany and Poland", whom he can only imagine. Although the most extensive of his Irish travels lay ahead of him, Swift already knew enough of the country, especially the rural backwaters which surrounded those islands of Protestant order, to understand the injustice as well as the impracticality of waste and oppression. Life in Ireland was beginning to teach Swift something about the grotesque side of civilisation.

In his regular correspondence with friends in England, Swift often laments the loss of a civilised society, and affects utter indifference to Irish affairs, even when we know that the evidence suggests quite a different picture. In January 1721, for example, in a letter to Alexander Pope, he harks back to those halcyon days with the Tories which ended with such tragic disillusionment, culminating in the death of Queen Anne:

> In a few weeks after the loss of that excellent Princess, I came to my station here; where I have continued ever since in the greatest privacy, and utter ignorance of those events which are most commonly talked of in the world; I neither know the Names nor Number of the Family which now reigns, further than the Prayer-book informs me. I cannot tell who is Chancellor, who are Secretaries, nor with what Nations we are in peace or war. And this manner of life was not taken up out of any sort of Affectation, but meerly to avoid giving offence, and for fear of provoking Party-zeal.

Yet we know that during these same years Swift hardly lived the life of a hermit. It is as if a new relationship with Ireland, sociable and engaged, was evidence of a kind of betrayal of England, and an unfortunate sign of a lowering of taste. This hiatus in his literary career seems to have done Swift all the good in the world, for we know that he was finding a new common cause with Ireland, and was quietly plotting ingenious satirical revenge on English political culture.

In April 1721, in a letter to Ford, Swift mentioned his latest literary enterprise:

> I am now writing a History of my Travells, which will be a large Volume, and gives Account of Countryes hitherto unknown; but they go on slowly for want of Health and Humor.

This is his first mention of *Gulliver's Travels*. Swift had conceived of an elaborate and provocative satire, based on the motif of a traveller's experience of remote cultures which might be of instructive value to civilised nations, a popular eighteenth-century genre of writing. He would spend almost five more years completing and revising his masterpiece.

4
A Tour of Munster

IN THE summer of 1723, Swift undertook and completed the most extensive and, in many ways, most dramatic tour of his life. He left Dublin in early June and travelled as far south as Cork, turned west, then headed for Galway, and returned to Dublin in early September. In those three months, he rode over five hundred miles, moving through three provinces. The statistics as well as the stamina are impressive enough, but most intriguing is the sense of a journey made for its own sake, without any of the usual social objectives. The mysterious character of this grand tour is intensified by Swift's near-complete silence: only one letter survives from this long absence, written to Thomas Sheridan near the end of his travels. He left few literary traces behind him, but folklore and anecdotal history have preserved several entertaining fictions about his movements that summer.

A popular version of Swift's decision to head south comes from a tragic reading of his romance with Vanessa, who had died on 2 June 1723, aged thirty-five. Late that night, Swift wrote a short letter to Chetwode, on a legal matter, which included the line, "I am forced to leave the town sooner than I expected", but specified no reason. He had undoubtedly heard of her death, but had no wish to be part of her funeral train. Obsessed with preserving the secrecy of their intimacy, he must have decided that a summer journey already contemplated

Swift's Expedition in the Summer of 1723

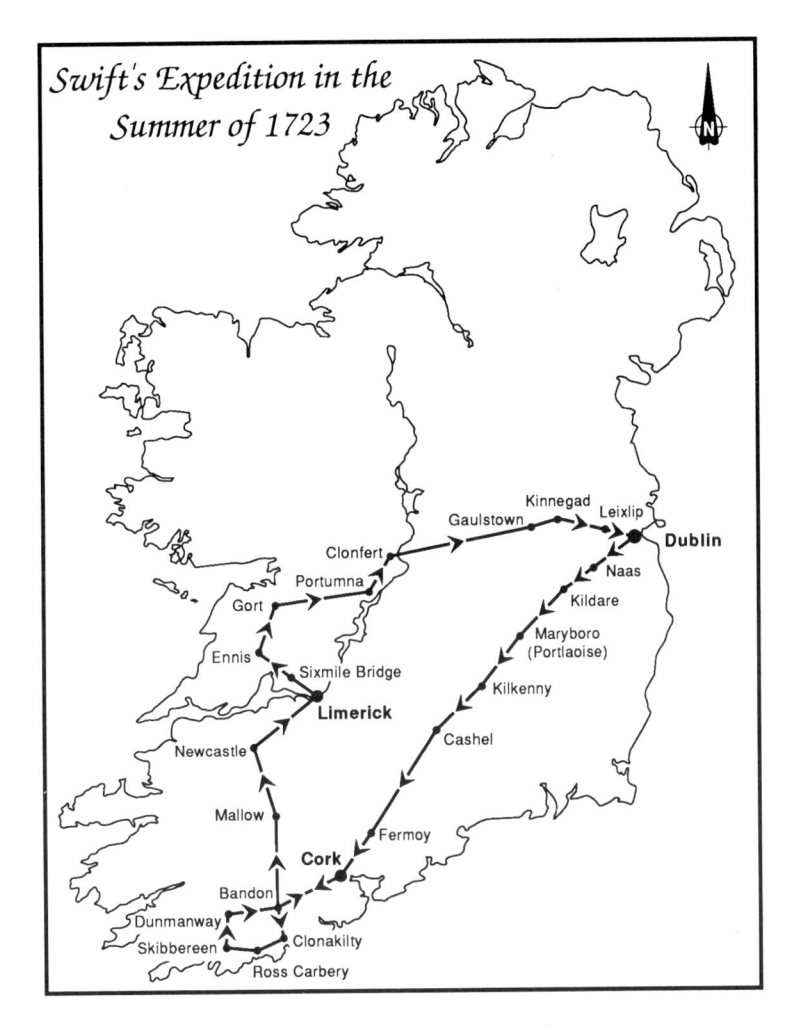

should be taken forthwith. Vanessa took her own secrets to the grave, and when her will was read, Swift was not even mentioned.

Personal tragedy and a planned retreat now coincided, and offered Swift an escape from Dublin which appeared as part of his customary summer's absence from the Deanery. But why did he turn south, since he had no close friends to visit in those unfamiliar territories, no host and family waiting to receive him? Whatever his reasons, Swift had repeatedly expressed a desire to make such an expedition. As far back as March 1715, he had told Chetwode that he would visit him shortly at Martry, his County Meath residence, "and thence if possible to Connaught and half around Ireland". In May 1719, in a letter to Vanessa, written entirely in romantic, if rather wooden, French, he repeated this intention to tour the South and the West. Finally, in May 1723, three weeks before Vanessa's death, he had written to Robert Cope, thanking him and his wife for their kindness and hospitality on his earlier visits, and then revealed his decision to explore new parts of the country:

> I will tell you that for some years I have intended a Southern journey; and this summer is fixed for it, and I hope to set out in ten days. I never was in those parts, nor am acquainted with one Christian among them, so that I shall be little more than a passenger; from thence I go to the Bishop of *Clonfert,* who expects me, and pretends to be prepared for me.

These lines suggest that Swift deliberately sought seclusion not company, adventure not familiarity, on his tour. The mention of the Bishop of Clonfert is an odd afterthought, since Swift had never been very friendly with the incumbent, Theophilus Bolton, who had earlier served as Swift's Chancellor at St Patrick's. Odder still, it seems as if Swift had simply invited himself, in order to enjoy a convenient stopping-off place, hardly a compliment to the bishop. In this letter to Cope, there is a touch of quiet bravado in Swift's saying he knows not "one Christian" in those parts he intends to visit. He will be, as the older sense of the word expresses it, a "passenger", someone always passing by, a civilised gypsy.

On 1 June, the eve of Vanessa's death, Swift had to write again to Cope, who seems not to have received the earlier letter. Swift had postponed his departure because a Dr Henry Jenny, a clergyman friend living at Mullaghbrack, outside Loughgall, had wished to accompany him on the tour. Swift now explains that he can wait no longer. Annoyed at the discourtesy as well as the delay, he repeats his simple plan:

> I go where I was never before, without one companion, and among people where I know no creature; and all this is to get a little exercise, for curing an ill head.

Since personal health is the standard reason for all Swift's travels, it sometimes sounds merely reflexive, even disingenuous, as it most certainly does here. A summer spent at Trim might have provided a less punishing remedy than an expedition to the extremes of Munster. On this occasion, it seems that Swift wanted to visit and explore unfamiliar landscapes, and was content that it would be a solitary pilgrimage.

Having made arrangements for Stella and Rebecca Dingley to stay with their mutual friend, Charles Ford, Swift left Dublin on 3 June and headed into the countryside. The early days of his ride south would not have been the least bit unfamiliar, let alone mysterious, since he was well used to the roads of Kildare, either the Galway road which led to the Rochforts, or the Limerick road which took him to Chetwode's estate. On this occasion, he would have taken the Limerick road to the county town of Maryborough (now Portlaoise), where the road divides, with one route continuing south-west to Limerick, while the other skirts the edge of Kilkenny and the entire length of Tipperary into Cork, the largest county in Ireland. Most commentators believe that Swift probably went through the ancient town of Cashel, County Tipperary, with its magnificent ruins of early mediaeval Ireland, and might have stayed at the bishop's palace there. Another reasonable possibility is that he came through the town of Kilkenny on his way south. This, after all, was the scene of his childhood, where he had been schooled for almost a decade. It was also an area where he had close family relatives, his uncle Godwin's estate, Swifte's Heath, lying only a few miles outside Kilkenny town. Would it not have been a haunting temptation for the fifty-five-year-old Dean to make the short detour to contemplate the site of his earliest years, a half-century beforehand? If he succumbed to this instinct to make a sentimental journey, he never mentioned it in print, literary romanticism of this kind not being part of his personality.

By several accounts, it seems that Swift passed through Cork city and stayed in the solidly Protestant town of Bandon, twenty miles to the south-west, sharing its name with the river on whose banks it is situated. Anecdote and folklore now complement, and sometimes replace, documentary evidence or factual information. It is said that when Swift arrived in Bandon, he saw inscribed on its walls the infamous lines, "A Turk, a Jew, or an Atheist may live in this Town, but no Papist", to which he replied with the following distich:

> He that wrote these lines did write them well,
> As the same is written on the gates of Hell.

After Bandon, he rode the thirteen miles down to the sea, to the town of Clonakilty, and from there proceeded along the rugged coast, with its succession of bays and inlets, until he came to the parish of Myross, five miles from Ross Carbery, on the road to Skibbereen.

This whole part of west Cork, at the southernmost tip of the country, was notable for its large number of Protestant estates. One of these was at Dunmanway, the seat of Sir Richard Cox, author of the controversial *Hibernia Anglicana* (1690), a defence of colonial plantation which had dismissed Gaelic historiography, such as Geoffrey Keating's *Foras Feasa ar Éirinn* (1630), as no more than wishful thinking, a series of naive fictions. Keating's work was itself an attempt to provide a dignified and systematic rebuttal of the colonist's propaganda, particularly that of Edmund Spenser's *A View of the Present State of Ireland* (1596). Although Swift had, once again, arrived safely in an outpost of English-speaking Ireland, he would not have been unaware of the native culture all around him. It was in this area that the Gaelic poetic tradition, the first vernacular literature in Europe, had developed in the eighth century, and whose current

From Geographical Description of Ye Kingdom of Ireland, *Petty and Lamb, c.1689.*

practitioners were now a threatened species desperately defending the integrity of their way of life against the supremacy of colonial rule. Along this same coastline, at Kinsale, over a century beforehand, the armies of Gaelic Ireland, under Hugh O'Neill of Tyrone, had been routed and humbled. In what came to be known as "the Flight of the Earls", the Irish leaders subsequently went into exile on the Continent and, in their absence, Ulster was systematically planted by the colonists.

Tradition has it that, while at Myross, Swift stayed with Rev. Philip Somerville, the local vicar. This detail is repeated by Edith Somerville and Martin Ross in their *Irish Memories* (1917), where they also record that the Dean spent much of his time at nearby Castletownshend, the seat of Colonel Bryan Townshend, from where he went on boating trips along the coast to Baltimore. While exploring this picturesque coastline, Swift apparently had to be rescued from the rocks by two servants, who delivered him safely. Perhaps by way of gratitude to the spirit of the place, he promptly composed a poetic tribute, "Carberiae Rupes", thirty-three lines of his best Latin, celebrating the wild delights of Ross Carbery. Swift never bothered to publish his evocation of this landscape, but his Latin original was later translated by a young Dublin poet, William Dunkin, a student at Trinity College, who created his own, inflated version of the Miltonic sublime:

> Lo! from the Top of yonder Cliff, that shrouds
> Its airy Head amidst the azure Clouds,
> Hangs a huge Fragment; destitute of props,
> Prone on the Waves the rocky Ruin drops.
> With hoarse Rebuff the swelling Seas rebound,
> From Shore to Shore the Rocks return the Sound:
> The dreadful Murmur Heav'n's high Convex cleaves,
> And *Neptune* shrinks beneath his Subject Waves;
> For, long the whirling Winds and beating Tides
> Had scoop'd a Vault into its nether Sides.
> Now yields the Base, the Summits nod, now urge
> Their headlong Course, and lash the sounding Surge.

"Carberiae Rupes" is Swift's only, and most unlikely, literary monument to his Munster tour. This was Swift the scholar-poet, deliberately choosing a language and a genre that would give his perspective a classical dignity, and which would also evoke those ancient poets, like his favourite Virgil, who escaped the city in order to embrace the unspoiled, innocent beauties of the countryside.

We do not know how long Swift stayed in County Cork, but Gaelic folklore and legend combine to indicate his path after Ross Carbery. Imaginative traces of his passage through parts of Kerry on his way to Limerick are found in several folktales which dramatise an encounter between Swift and Aogán Ó Rathaille, one of Ireland's greatest native poets of this period. Ó Rathaille, from the Sliabh Luachra area east of Killarney, was one of the last aristocratic poets of that Gaelic world, now

Muckross Abbey, County Kerry, from Antiquities of Ireland, *by Francis Grose, 2 Vols., London, 1791–95.*

reduced to beggary and nostalgia. His own patrons, the Brownes, had seen their estates confiscated after 1690, and could no longer afford to maintain the poet. The following tale, collected in the early years of this century, comes from the Beare peninsula in south-west Kerry:

> It is said that Dean Swift travelled Ireland in order to find out which County had the most learned inhabitants. The Kerry people heard that he was coming, and they asked Aogán Ó Rathaille to face him. Aogán dressed himself up like a cowherd, with a rope around his waist and two mangy dogs running at his heels, and placed himself on the road which the Dean would be travelling.
>
> Once Swift came within earshot, Aogán commenced to speak Latin to one of his cows, Greek to another, and hard rhetorical Irish to another still. He was proceeding to more cows and other languages when Dean Swift turned to his servant and said in amazement:
>
> 'The cowherds here in Kerry speak seven languages! What, then, must the scholars be like? It is no use for me to compete with them!'
>
> And, turning on his heel, he headed straight back to Dublin without delay.

Such folktales cover over the darker historical background which links these two artists, one of whom dreamed of a Jacobite restoration, while the other endorsed the dispossession of Catholic Ireland. Ó Rathaille's world was in chronic decline, while that of Swift, though still not entirely free of political anxiety, was consolidating its new conquests. Ó Rathaille died in 1729, six years after Swift's tour of Munster, and was buried at Muckross Abbey, by the lakes of Killarney.

The next sighting of Swift was in County Clare, just above the widening estuary of the River Shannon, north of the city of Limerick. Legend has the Dean stopping overnight in the village of Sixmilebridge. On enquiring for his evening meal in a tavern, Swift was told that meat was unavailable, Friday being a fast-day for Catholics. He noticed the local Catholic bishop seated at a neighbouring table, and asked the landlady to pass the clerical dignitary the following impromptu verses:

> Can any man of common sense
> Think eating meat gives God offence,
> Or that the herring hath a charm
> The Almighty's anger to disarm?
> Wrapt up in majesty divine
> Does he reflect on what we dine?

The bishop, delighted by the Dean's wit, commanded meat for his Protestant companion, and an imagined friendship concludes the tale. Still heading north, Swift would have passed the mediaeval splendours of Bunratty and Dromoland castles on the short road to Ennis, then crossed the Slieve Aughty mountains to reach Portumna, in County Galway, on the north shore of Lough Derg. After another fifteen miles, following the banks of the Shannon, he would have arrived at the small, but important, cathedral of Clonfert, to the south of Ballinasloe, and called, gratefully, to the palace of Bishop Theophilus Bolton. (The bishop's palace, a long, two-storied residence situated behind the cathedral, was occupied until the 1950s,

The Hiberno-Romanesque doorway of Clonfert Cathedral. The bishop's palace lay in the grounds behind the cathedral. (Courtesy of the Office of Public Works)

after which it fell into ruin.) There is an appropriate conjunction between Swift's travels and the historical legend of Clonfert Cathedral. As "Cluain Fhearta Bhrendáin", the Gaelic name for the place indicates, this is the site of monastic Ireland's greatest traveller, St Brendan, the sixth-century monk who supposedly discovered America in one of his epic voyages across the Atlantic.

The single, surviving letter from this journey is dated

3 August 1723, and was sent by Swift from Clonfert to Sheridan, at Quilca, County Cavan. There is no indication of how long he has been with the bishop, but he sounds as if he is glad to be stationary for a while, telling his friend, "I am half weary with the four hundred I have rode". Swift also includes his customary report on a host's attention to the land and its improvement, praising Bolton for having dug "twelve Miles of Ditches from his House to the Shannon". This letter sounds like a reply to one sent to Clonfert ahead of his arrival, since he declines an invitation from Sheridan to pass by Quilca on his way home to Dublin, saying, "No, I cannot possibly be with you so soon, there are too many Rivers, Bogs, and Mountains between." Swift had clearly decided that he would now return home, but added, "I shall make one or two short Visits in my way to Dublin." Whenever he left Bolton, he would have crossed the Shannon into County Offaly, and from there directly into County Westmeath, familiar territory from the time of his several visits to the Rochforts.

The final miles of the road back into Dublin would have been rich in familiar sights and images for Swift, passing through the towns of Maynooth and Leixlip, with Celbridge only a couple of miles off the main road, then meeting the city boundary, the expanding Phoenix Park to the left, the Royal Hospital at Kilmainham to the right and, finally, having climbed sharply up into the streets of St Patrick's Liberties, his Irish Odyssey was complete.

While Swift was away, Stella and Rebecca Dingley had enjoyed the comfort and hospitality of Charles Ford's home, an old castellated mansion in the Norman style, surrounded by one hundred and twenty acres of rich pastureland, just outside Dunboyne, only eleven miles from the capital. In a humorous and playful poem, "Stella at Woodpark", Swift, like a father come to collect his children, tells of calling to the estate to see a friend now spoilt by the aristocratic leisure of life in the country:

Leixlip Castle, on the River Liffey, from Fisher's Scenery of Ireland *(1795).*

> The winter sky began to frown,
> Poor Stella must pack off to town.
> From purling streams and fountains bubbling,
> To Liffey's stinking tide in Dublin.

The indulgent Ford will now be replaced by the stricter Swift, who sympathises with poor Stella's disappointment when forced to return to the ordinariness of a spinster's lodging on Ormonde Quay. Yet, earlier in the year, Swift had written a birthday-poem for Ford in which he portrayed the city in a very positive light. In that poem, written in the form of friendly advice, he urges Ford, too often an absentee in London, to appreciate the superior attractions of his native city:

> Can you on Dublin look with scorn?
> Yet here were you and Ormonde born.
> Oh, were but you and I so wise
> To look with Robin Grattan's eyes:
> Robin adores that spot of earth,

That literal spot which gave him birth,
And swears, Cushogue is to his taste,
As fine as Hampton Court at least.

Swift's evolving patriotism is hinted at in his own marginal note to his copy of the poem, where he glosses "Cushogue" as "the true (Irish) name of Belcamp". He could now point out Ford's unnatural and unhealthy snobbery about Ireland all the more tolerantly since he suffered from the very same defect. When corresponding with English friends, he often emphasised his identification with them by denying any for Ireland. But within his Irish circle of friends, drawn almost exclusively from the Protestant minority, he regularly attacked an irrational and degrading anglophilia which, he argued, was unworthy as well as absurd. Having aimed for, and been denied, a lasting career in England, Swift could understand, with bitter amusement, how foolish it was for Irishmen to entertain such ambition. He came to recommend the patriotic and psychological good sense of Caesar's remark, that "he would rather be the *first* Man, in I know not what Village, than the *second* in *Rome*". Swift's attitudes towards both England and Ireland, his oft-declared love of one and loathing for the other, are sometimes created for effect, are not so predictable or as consistent as we might expect, and undergo significant change during his lifetime.

One of the most fascinating questions about Swift's literary career during these years is the nature of the influence of his own travels upon *Gulliver's Travels*. That it was partly intended as a form of imaginative revenge upon English politics and politicians is generally accepted. But does the fact that the story was conceived and refined in Ireland influence the work? We know, from Swift's own letters, that the Voyages to Lilliput and Brobdingnag were already written by the summer of 1722, and that the most controversial section, Part IV, set in the land of the Houyhnhnms, was finished by the end of the following year. This means that, whatever Swift had designed and drafted for

The demesne of Lucan, on the River Liffey, from Fisher's Scenery of Ireland *(1795). Lucan and Leixlip were popular and stylish spas in the eighteenth century. Less than ten miles from Dublin, both places were very familiar to Swift.*

the allegorical tale of his civilised horses and bestial Yahoos, this part of the satire was completed after his tour of Munster. All those weeks spent alone, riding through strange and wonderful new scenes, some sublime, others ghastly, seeing and hearing a distressed and often incomprehensible peasantry in between those sanctuaries of Anglican order and refinement – all this experience must have entered into, and helped to shape, the imaginative contours of Swift's fantasy.

In January 1724, four months after his tour of Munster, Swift wrote to Ford, who was once again in London, in his Pall Mall apartments:

> My greatest want here is of somebody qualifyed to censure and correct what I write, I know not above two or three whose Judgement I would value, and they are lazy, negligent, and without any Opinion of my Abilityes. I have left the Country of Horses, and am in the flying Island, where I shall not stay long, and my two last Journeys will be soon over....

His *Travels* were nearly complete, save for the Voyage to Laputa, "the flying Island", which would preoccupy him for quite a while yet. After the most adventurous journey of his life, taken to foreign parts of his own island, Swift had withdrawn for the winter into the discipline of his utopian dream.

5

Quilca, County Cavan

SPENDING the entire summer away from Dublin, often in the company of a rural gentry or clergy who were both tolerant and lively, soon became a ritual outing for Swift. If, however, he had sought no more than domestic comfort and social elegance, the literary record of these visits probably would amount to no more than a series of polite tributes to hospitality. Naturally, Swift warmed to civilised surroundings, but his observant energy and imaginative curiosity ensured that he saw, and responded to, much more than the drawing-rooms of respectable hosts.

In 1722, Swift had spent nearly six months in Ulster, visiting several friends, John Stearne at Clogher, Robert Cope MP at Loughgall, Robert Lindsay MP at Cookstown and, for the first time, Thomas Sheridan at Quilca, County Cavan. Most of our information about his movements that summer comes from the several letters he wrote to Vanessa, still housebound at Celbridge. Writing from Loughgall in July, he tells her that the bad weather has kept him indoors, reading "diverting Books of History and Travells". On the other hand, it seems that he had been exceptionally active and adventurous in the previous weeks, declaring, "I have shifted Scenes oftener than ever I did in my Life, and I believe, have layn in thirty Beds since I left the Toun. . . ." One of Swift's most telling remarks about the landscape around Loughgall, and the way it contrasts with most of the country, comes in a letter to Charles Ford, written at the end of July. After the usual complaint about atrocious weather hindering his daily exercise, he remarks:

> My Comfort is, that the People, the Churches and the Plantations make me think I am in England. I mean onely the Scene of a few miles about me, for I have passed through miserable Regions to get to it.

Such orderliness pleased and reassured him, but it did not arouse his imagination. Although he ventured as far west as Fermanagh to witness what he called "the longest Lake in Ireland", Lough Erne, and declared a fancy to visit "the broadest", Lough Neagh, the visit to Loughgall itself seems to have provided Swift with everything except interest and activity, and he complained to Ford, "Here are neither extraordinary Scenes of Art or of Nature". Cope himself, a good friend of both Ford and Chetwode, is described by Swift, with neither enthusiasm nor displeasure, as "the most domestick man you ever saw". Despite these reservations, Swift stayed at Loughgall for five weeks and left on 7 August, heading south towards Quilca, where he would meet Sheridan who, at the same time, was travelling up from Dublin.

The day after he left the Cope family, Swift wrote again to Vanessa, telling her that he had ridden twenty-eight miles on his first day, and adding:

> Here I leave this Letter to travel one way while I go another, but where I do not know, nor what Cabbins or Bogs are in my Way.

This sounds, misleadingly, as if he was content to wander aimlessly. In a land where, as Swift puts it, "Politeness is as much a Stranger as Cleanlyness", not to know where you were, nor where your destination lay, could be more dangerous than arduous. We do not know which route he took from Loughgall, but whether he went directly south through the wilds of Monaghan, or along the more familiar road through Newry, Dundalk and Ardee, he would have ridden at least fifty miles to

Loughgall Manor, County Armagh, from an early twentieth-century photograph by H. Allison.

reach Quilca. This inaugural visit to County Cavan brought him into earthy contact with the most enjoyable, and the most frustrating, company of his many travels.

Quilca is a townland outside Virginia, an old planter town on the shores of Lough Ramor, in the south-eastern corner of the county, taking its name from the Irish "cuilceach", meaning a place abundant with reeds. It lies just eight miles from Kells, one of the principal towns in the bordering county of Meath. Thomas Sheridan's small estate had been inherited through his wife, Elizabeth, née McFadden. The couple had seven children, including the famous actor and theatre-manager, Thomas, one of Swift's earliest biographers and father of the playwright Richard Brinsley. Swift admired Sheridan, twenty years his junior, for his wit and learning, calling him "the best instructor of youth in these kingdoms, or perhaps in Europe", but pitied him on account of his shrewish wife and demanding brood of children. For most of the year, Sheridan ran his classical academy in Capel Street, Dublin, on the other side of the Liffey from St Patrick's, retiring to Quilca during the summer months.

Swift seems to have stayed for several weeks during this 1722 visit, since the next surviving letter of this year, to Robert Cope, was written in early October, and talks of having "just come to town" after his northern trip. It is possible that Swift wrote to nobody while staying with Sheridan, although such a silence would be most unusual for so energetic a correspondent. In a letter written to Sheridan in late December, Swift recalls Quilca with teasing nostalgia for summer escapades spent together:

> You will find Quilca not the Thing it was last *August*; nobody to relish the Lake; nobody to ride over the Downs; no Trout to be caught; no dining over a Well; no Night Heroics, no Morning Epics; no Stollen Hour when the Wife is gone; no Creature to call you Names. Poor miserable Master *Sheridan*! No blind Harpers! no Journies to *Rantavan*!

From this very first image of life at Quilca, which celebrates a rare kind of youthful freedom and spontaneity in an otherwise supremely ordered life, Swift always associated the place with a domestic anarchy which beggared civilised belief. It was also a place which offered a liberating and challenging primitivism, one which aroused Swift's literary humour. With these memories of "Night Heroics" and "blind Harpers", the fifty-four-year-old Dean conjures up an Ireland of which he should not have approved, but one which clearly delighted his fancy. The combination of domestic ruin and cultural refinement makes Sheridan seem more like one of those Gaelic hedge-school masters than an Anglican clergyman. After the orderly delights of Gaulstown and Woodbrooke, Quilca offered real abandon, with a host who could introduce him to people and places he would normally never encounter. Whenever Swift is at Quilca, he seems closer to "native" Ireland than in any other company: this has possibly something to do with the fact that the Sheridans were Catholics up to around 1600, when Thomas's grandfather, Denis, converted to Protestantism, later helping Bishop Bedell to translate the Bible into Irish.

Over the next three years, the pilgrimage to Quilca became an annual affair which also included "the Ladies", Stella and

Rebecca Dingley. Swift and his companions spent Christmas 1723 at Sheridan's home, and stayed on into January. He was convinced that the country air and a regimen of daily exercise would mend Stella's weak constitution. This caring belief was severely tested by the seemingly appalling conditions at Quilca which, according to Swift's imaginative, usually satirical, version of the place, promised to destroy both the faith and well-being of any Christian. The Dean began an outlandish fictional catalogue about this chaotic residence, "The Blunders, Deficiences, Distresses, and Misfortunes of Quilca", in which he enumerated the barbarous conditions for gentle guests:

> Not a Bit of Turf this cold Weather, and Mrs Johnson and the Dean in Person, with all their Servants forced to assist at the Bog in gathering up the wet Bottoms of old Clamps.

In this grotesque and absurd version of a pastoral idyll, the guests are reduced to the class of field-labourers. Everything that might go wrong does go wrong, and all is blamed, unsurprisingly, on idle and cunning servants. "The Blunders" is a literary composition whose humorous conception softens the dogged iteration of relentless and ingenious humiliation. Quilca's vast potential for farce is noted by Swift in a mock-literary subtitle to this sketch, in which he proposes a weekly instalment leading, eventually, to "one and twenty Volumes in Quarto". It has often been pointed out that such versions of Anglo-Irish country living anticipate the Big House world of Maria Edgeworth's *Castle Rackrent* (1800), in which the squirearchy, having abandoned all hope of decorum and normality, are almost indistinguishable from the servants.

Shortly after Swift and the ladies returned to Dublin in early 1724, he became embroiled in a public controversy which kept him in Dublin for most of the year. In April, he wrote to Charles Ford who was, once again, in London:

Lough Ramor, Virginia, County Cavan, a late eighteenth-century engraving printed by W. Allen in Dublin. (Courtesy of the National Library of Ireland)

I do not know whether I told you that I sent a small Pamphlet under the Name of a Draper, laying the whole Vilany open, and advising People what to do; about 2000 of them have been dispersed by Gentlemen in severall Parts of the Country, but one can promise nothing from such Wretches as the Irish People.

This was the first clear signal of what was to become Swift's most famous literary engagement with Irish affairs, that of "Wood's half-pence", in which he joined, then inspired, and finally led, a national protest against the grant of a patent to an Englishman, William Wood, to coin money for Ireland. Through the persona of the Drapier, Swift denounced arbitrary rule and asserted Ireland's constitutional independence. Using the simple and popular pseudonym of this Dublin tradesman, he wrote six pamphlets during 1724, each one intensifying public interest in the legal and political implications of the affair. London became so concerned that the Lord Lieutenant, the Duke of Grafton, was quickly replaced by John Carteret who, it was hoped, would soon resolve the issue.

For the first time since becoming Dean, Swift assumed the role of spokesman for, and defender of, the constitutional and political rights of Protestant Ireland. Having worked at the heart of the English political system, he also had the knowledge and the experience of imperial power to strengthen his attack on English hypocrisy in dealing with its loyal subjects in Ireland. In the third pamphlet of the campaign, which appeared in September, addressed to *The Nobility and Gentry of the Kingdom of Ireland*, the Drapier asked a series of provocatively innocent questions:

> Were not the People of *Ireland* born as *free* as those of *England*? How have they forfeited their Freedom? Is not their *Parliament* as fair a *Representative* of the *People*, as that of *England*? And hath not their Privy Council as great, or a greater Share in the Administration of publick Affairs? Are they not Subjects of the same King? Does not the same *Sun* shine over them? And have they not the same *God* for their Protector? Am I a *Free-man* in *England*, and do I become a *Slave* in six Hours, by crossing the Channel?

Questions like these, which appeal to Irish patriotism while confronting the English administration without fear or servility, could be conceived and delivered only by someone absolutely sure of the simple integrity of his cause. *The Drapier's Letters* represent a carefully orchestrated pattern of demands, lessons and appeals aimed at all those in Ireland who were committed to the country's legislative independence and economic prosperity.

Swift's personal commitment to the campaign against Wood's half-pence may be heard in the daring rhetoric of the Drapier, but also seen in the fact that, for the first time in years, he stayed in Dublin throughout the summer and autumn, keen to be at the heart of changing events. In a letter to Ford, written in mid-June, he explained this most unusual situation, partly in terms of civic loyalty, partly in terms of domestic necessity:

> I am kept from my usuall summer travelling, by building a Wall, which will ruin both my Health and Fortune, as well as humor.

This monumental undertaking was a high wall to enclose a large tract of ground to the south of the Deanery, given the biblical name of "Naboth's Vineyard" by Swift, who wanted to develop it as a garden and shelter. Such an improvement, he argued, would protect his fruit trees from harsh winds and secure a safe grazing area for his horses. When he was not engaged with his Drapier's pamphlets, he spent all his energy supervising this project, telling Knightley Chetwode, "I am over head and ears in mortar, and with a number of the greatest rogues in Ireland, which is a proud word." In November, at the height of a sensational court-case, in which Swift's printer, John Harding, was charged with the treasonable sentiments of the Drapier, Swift told Ford that the wall was now complete, and lamented the cost of £400. For Swift, the vexing irony of the whole project was that he had also paid a severe price for his poor health, which the absence of a holiday had aggravated.

Determined to have some kind of break from Dublin to restore his spirits, Swift told Ford that he was going to the country "to try new Air for a few days". This turned out to be three weeks spent at Belcamp with the Grattans, from the last few days of November to mid-December. While there, he wrote his sixth pamphlet on the Wood's half-pence controversy, still employing the mask of a Drapier, and entitled it *A Letter to the Right Honourable the Lord Viscount Molesworth*. Robert Molesworth was a prominent Irish Whig, noted for his defence of Irish legislative independence. His estate lay at Brackdenstown, just outside Swords, only a few miles from Belcamp. In the pamphlet, the Drapier praises Molesworth for his patriotism, and concludes with a playful image of himself and his horse visiting the home of this worthy statesman:

> Since your last Residence in *Ireland*, I frequently have taken my Nag to ride about your Grounds; where I fancied myself to feel an Air of *Freedom* breathing round me. . . . But I have lately sold my Nag, and honestly told his greatest Fault, which was that of snuffing up the Air about

Brackdenstown; whereby he became such a Lover of *Liberty*, that I could scarce hold him in.

A keen student of horseflesh, Swift would have enjoyed working this image of natural and instinctive freedom into the conversational style of the pamphlet. In the Irish political context, such an image is forced to suffer from ironic distortion, as indeed do most features of the landscape: the Drapier's nag finds freedom so unusual as to be unnatural. Having been intoxicated by his new-found liberty, the poor animal is no longer fit or worthy to serve his disappointed master.

One of the several ironies of this controversy was that, while the Drapier continued to expose the arrogance and wickedness of the English administration of Ireland, Swift courted the friendship of that administration's representative, Lord Lieutenant Carteret. In April 1725, Swift wrote a careful and gracious letter to Carteret, requesting him to use his good offices to secure a suitable clerical promotion for Thomas Sheridan, who was already one of Carteret's domestic chaplains. He praises Sheridan's cultural learning and educational talents, but laments that "His greatest Fault is a Wife and seven Children, for which there is no excuse but that a Wife is thought necessary to a Schoolmaster." Swift hoped that the Lord Lieutenant would help to rescue his friend from an economic and personal drudgery largely the result of his own feckless personality, as opposed to the usual scapegoat of wife and children. In the same letter, he informs Carteret that he is "hasting into the Country to try what Exercise and better Air will do" for his poor health. Swift was heading back with the ladies to Quilca, which Sheridan had lent him as a rural retreat while he himself continued working at his school in Dublin.

Swift spent the next six months at Quilca, his longest-ever stay there. In his correspondence that summer, nothing much seems to have changed in his view of the place and its inhabitants:

> The weather has been so unfavourable, and continues so, that I have not been able to ride above once, and have been forced for amusement to set Irish fellows to work, and to oversee them. I live in a cabin and in a very wild country; yet there are some agreeablenesses in it, or at least I fancy so, and am levelling mountains and raising stones, and fencing against inconveniences of a scanty lodging, want of victuals, and a thievish race of people.

This scene, from a letter to Chetwode written in May, is the familiar one of merry anarchy in which everything and everyone, from the climate to the cook, conspire to ruin his holiday. In the midst of all, there is the Dean himself, almost a Gulliver, trying to civilise the intractable earth, with his talk of "levelling mountains and raising stones". Yet there were some "agreeablenesses" about the experience, otherwise he would hardly have stayed for almost three seasons of that year.

His own health and that of Stella seem to have benefited from the rigours of Quilca, but Rebecca Dingley hated the place, preferring, as Swift puts it, to "live in a Dublin cellar, than in a country palace". Despite the dreadful weather, the wet turf, the scheming servants and the draughty house, Swift thrived on the challenge to his constitution and, in a letter to Sheridan at the end of June, poeticised succinctly what he entitled "The Blessings of a Country Life":

> Far from our Debtors,
> No Dublin Letters,
> Not seen by our Betters.

The sentiment of that middle line is quite fanciful, since Swift posted and collected letters from nearby Kells every Saturday, many of them concerning the running of his cathedral. From these, we learn that the cost of the wall behind the Deanery still rankled, as did the probable effect which the rainy summer would have on the apple-trees and the hay in Naboth's Vineyard. Always a poetical subversive, Swift could not resist adding "The Plagues of a Country Life" to the letter:

> A companion without news,
> A great want of shoes;
> Eat lean meat, or choose;
> A church without pews,
> Our horses astray,
> No straw, oats or hay;
> December in May,
> Our boys run away,
> All servants at play.

Such is the inescapable ambiguity of so many of Swift's versions of places like Quilca, it is hard, perhaps fruitless, to decide as to which one is closest to his true feelings.

While Swift was at Quilca, his absent friend and host had the good fortune to secure Carteret's favour. Thanks to Swift's intervention, Sheridan was appointed to the parish of Rincurran, at Kinsale, County Cork. The distance from Dublin as well as from Cavan dismayed Swift, who called it "a Living the furthest in the Kingdom from Quilca". Sheridan was no sooner installed in his new living, however, than he preached a politically inappropriate sermon, beginning with the lines from the Sermon on the Mount, "Sufficient unto the day is the evil thereof", which seemed to betray disloyalty to the Hanoverian succession. After an uproar by leading Irish Whigs, Carteret was obliged to dismiss him as chaplain, and Sheridan was stigmatised as a cunning Jacobite. Swift, ever-loyal to his younger friend, consoled him by saying it was virtuous innocence, and not political stupidity, which caused this unfortunate episode, and urged him yet again to instil some order into his affairs.

Swift's major preoccupation this summer lay with the still unresolved issue of Wood's half-pence. Just as he followed every stage of Sheridan's personal drama from his Quilca retreat, so too he kept in close touch with a national controversy which had created enormous excitement and tension in the country. It was common knowledge in Dublin that the Dean of St Patrick's was the author of *The Drapier's Letters*, but nobody would publicly denounce or expose him: a reward of £300, offered by Dublin Castle for information leading to the arrest of the author, was never claimed.

While the capital was preparing for the opening of parliament, to take place on 7 September, Swift wrote yet another pamphlet, *An Humble Address to Both Houses of Parliament*, which he hoped to publish on the very same day. In this latest intervention, the seventh on the issue, the Drapier appealed to the Irish politicians to assert the authority and sovereignty of their institution. He used the occasion to remind his audience that no nation could prosper without control over its own affairs, and listed the many reforms that the parliament should attend to urgently, especially afforestation, the promotion of tillage, and a more systematic use of natural resources, such as the bogs. He concluded his appeal with a characteristic realism born out of scepticism:

> ... few *Politicians*, with all their Schemes, are half so useful Members of a Commonwealth, as an *honest Farmer*; who, by skilfully draining, fencing, manuring and planting, hath increased the intrinsick Value of a Piece of Land; and thereby done a *perpetual Service* to his Country; which it is a great Controversy, whether any of the *former* ever did, since the Creation of the World; but no Controversy at all, that Ninety-nine in a Hundred, have done Abundance of Mischief.

Thomas Sheridan. Signed "Cook", this engraving is probably by the London artist Thomas Cook (1744–1818), who executed many such portraits for literary publications. (Courtesy of the National Library of Ireland)

While showing the Drapier's practical understanding of patriotism, in which the farmer is elevated above the politician, the passage cannot resist belittling those very politicians to whom it so earnestly appeals. This tension between hope and despair lay at the heart of many of Swift's Irish pamphlets: he needed to rebuke, but increasingly doubted its value.

Drafted and finished at Quilca, the pamphlet was brought

From Geographical Description of Ye Kingdom of Ireland, *Petty and Lamb, c.1689.*

down to Dublin by Jack Grattan who, along with others, softened some of the more provocative points in the text. This interference annoyed Swift, who referred contemptuously to such censorship as "cowardly caution". Staying at Quilca, while entrusting friends to deal with the printer in Dublin, meant that Swift had to sacrifice ultimate control of the publication. However, the exercise suddenly became academic when Carteret announced that the original patent granted to Wood had been officially withdrawn. The minute Swift heard the news, he penned a short letter to John Worrall, his choirmaster at St Patrick's:

> Since Wood's patent is cancelled, it will by no means be convenient to have the paper printed, as I suppose you, and Jack Grattan, and Sherridan [*sic*] will agree; therefore, if it be with the printer, I would have it taken back, and the press broke.... The work is done, and there is no more need of the Drapier.

Swift's businesslike tone here gives no sense of the popular delight and satisfaction felt throughout the colony on hearing the news of the government's climbdown. Protestant Ireland celebrated a rare triumph over the English administration: in Dublin, the bells of St Patrick's were rung, bonfires were lit, and effigies of the heroic Drapier were paraded victoriously through the streets.

Shortly before the triumphant outcome of the Drapier's campaign, and in a tactical move designed to warn the government of the power of popular discontent, several leading citizens of Dublin ensured that the Corporation carried a motion proclaiming the Dean of St Patrick's a Freeman of the City. It was not until 1730, however, that the Lord Mayor and the Common Council approved of payment for a gold box, "the value thereof not to exceed twenty five pounds", to symbolise the city's gratitude. Irritated by this tardy tribute, Swift demanded that a fitting inscription be engraved on the box, and secretly composed one himself, getting his friend Patrick Delany to copy and then deliver it to the Council. Some of the aldermen were unhappy about the way Swift was trying to dictate the terms of the dedication, and an unresolved political squabble about the wording ensued. On 27 May, the Lord Mayor and aldermen arrived at the Deanery to make formal presentation of the box, still uninscribed. Swift used the occasion to lecture his captive dignitaries on their petty ignorance and crawling venality. He kept the box, however, and treasured it until his death, when it was bequeathed to a friend, Alexander McAulay, a Dublin judge.

During this prolonged stay at Quilca, Swift was working away on one of the most famous utopian tales the world has ever known. Despite the uncivil domestic conditions, his continued activity as the Drapier, and a regular correspondence with friends in Ireland and England, Swift found time to finish the major satire he had been writing for five years. In August 1725, he told Ford:

> I have finished my Travells, and I am now transcribing them; they are admirable Things, and will wonderfully mend the World.

Travels into Several Remote Parts and Nations of the World, later called, simply, *Gulliver's Travels*, was nearly ready for publication. Several friends, including Sheridan, had already been shown extracts. In September, when Swift wrote to reassure his friend after the row over the sermon, he told him not to upset himself about the irrationality of people's behaviour, and illustrated his point with an image of "natural" ignorance and stupidity drawn from his new story:

> Therefore sit down and be quiet, and mind your Business as you should do, and contract your Friendships, and expect no more from Man than such an Animal is capable of, and you will every day find my Description of Yahoes more resembling.

Swift's image of the war between barbarity and civilisation was nurtured and transformed by his own experience of being, or trying to remain, a gentleman in a land whose way of life he often found loathsome and incomprehensible. Gulliver discovered the Yahoos on the other side of the globe; Swift found them beyond Finglas.

Towards the end of his stay, Swift completed his caricature of Sheridan's home in the verses "To Quilca", in which the familiar imagery of perverse disorder and unnatural confusion reappears:

> Through all the valleys, hills, and plains,
> The goddess Want in triumph reigns;
> And her chief officers of state,
> Sloth, Dirt, and Theft around her wait.

These fanciful sprites of a grotesque pastoral are a characteristic element of Swift's well-established and ongoing literary banter with Sheridan. One of the most creative and energetic periods of his literary career coincides with what he would have us believe was merely a battle against inconvenience.

The Dean and the ladies returned to Dublin in early October 1725. The city welcomed back its most celebrated son, who was pleased to see the first edition of *The Drapier's Letters*, entitled *Fraud Detected; Or, The Hibernian Patriot*, printed by an enterprising young Dubliner, George Faulkner, whose reputation was eventually secured when, in 1735, he would publish the first edition of Swift's *Works*. Despite the adulation which marked his homecoming, the Dean seems to have been deeply depressed to be back in the city after such a long residence in the country. At the end of November, answering a letter from a friend, James Stopford, who was touring France, Swift headed his reply with the rather melodramatic address, "Wretched Dublin, in miserable Ireland", and went on to describe himself as "the Dean of St Patrick's sitting like a toad in a corner of his great house, with a perfect hatred of all public actions and persons". He envied Stopford's freedom and leisure, and mockingly rebuked him for sending so little news, "What have *vous autres voyageurs* to do but write and ramble?" To finish this self-conscious complaint, he added:

> Take care of your health, and come home by Switzerland; from whence travel blindfold till you get here, which is the only way to make Ireland tolerable.

Presumably, the benefit of the blindfold is to avoid seeing the beauties of the English landscape en route to Ireland, a vision that would torture him when he was back "home": for someone serving a life-sentence, he suggests, freedom is a delight best denied. It had been over a decade since Swift himself had seen England, an ancestral country becoming increasingly remote as a reality, but one which continued to serve as an imaginative contrast to the more familiar landscapes of his birthplace. Having finished transcribing his new book, Swift now made plans to sail to England in order to make arrangements with an unsuspecting London publisher to deliver himself of his comic, if nightmarish, masterpiece of satirical fantasy.

6

The Irish Sea

THE INTERESTS and demands of Swift's religious and literary career, and his enduring attachment to English friends, ensured that he became an experienced, if reluctant, sea-traveller. During his lifetime, Swift crossed the Irish Sea on more than twenty occasions, which reflects not just his continuous preoccupation with English affairs, political and personal, but a remarkable and fearless energy. The journey could take as little as a day in fine weather, or as long as three days in stormy conditions, and was usually an endurance test for travellers, never a simple pleasure. It was an elemental experience, often a dangerous one, which must have reinforced Swift's sense of Ireland as an isolated outpost, an island much further away from Wales than the modern experience or imagination might understand.

Sea travel had a traumatic childhood association for Swift, one that seems to have lasted for most of his life, as he explained in the detached style of an autobiographical fragment written in his old age:

> He was born in Dublin on St Andrews day, and when he was a year old, an event happened to him that seems very unusuall; for his Nurse who was a woman of Whitehaven, being under an absolute necessity of seeing one of her relations, who was then extremely sick, and from whom she expected a Legacy; and being at the same time extremely fond of the infant, she stole him on shipboard unknown to his Mother and Uncle, and carryed him with her to Whitehaven, where

Holyhead Collegiate Church on the Isle of Anglesey, by Samuel and Nathaniel Buck, London, 1742. Note the three packet-boats, one of them under sail from the bay. (Courtesy of the National Library of Wales)

he continued for almost three years. For when the matter was discovered, His Mother sent orders by all means not to hazard a second voyage, till he could be better able to bear it. The nurse was so carefull of him that before he returned he had learnt to spell, and by the time that he was three years old he could read any chapter in the Bible.

Swift had been abducted from his home and forced to undertake the long journey north-east, in a sea notorious at the time for piracy, to the coast of Cumberland, just below Carlisle. Like the homunculus Gulliver in the land of the King of Brobdingnag, this image of the captive child surviving his first passage across the sea must have both fascinated and horrified Swift.

We have considerable detail about Swift's subsequent voyages, some of it from his personal account-books, which noted the precise costs of each journey, some from his letters, either planning or recounting a trip. All such voyages across the Irish Sea were taken aboard "packet-boats", so-called because they usually carried the Royal Mail as well as passengers. These boats, sometimes referred to as "yachts", usually sailed three times a week between Ringsend, south of Dublin Bay, and either Holyhead, in Anglesey, Wales, or Parkgate, on the River Dee, near Chester. Ringsend, where Cromwell had landed with his Irish expeditionary force in 1649, was the nearest point on the Liffey estuary where such boats could safely dock, as the bay

Chester Castle and the Dee Bridge, by Francis Place (1647–1728). In 1698, Place came to Ireland and spent a year travelling around the country, painting and drawing a variety of scenes. Much of that work can now be seen in the National Gallery of Ireland. (Courtesy of the Board of Trustees of the Victoria and Albert Museum)

around the city was still too shallow for these vessels. Disembarking at the other end of the journey could be unpredictable, and special labourers were sometimes employed at Holyhead to carry passengers on their backs through the last few hundred feet to dry shore. Once landed safely, travellers had to endure a journey of nearly one hundred miles across the coast road through Bangor and Conway before they reached their first English town, Chester, where they could rest themselves and their horses, before facing the remaining one hundred and eighty miles to London.

In all his travels, whether by land or sea, Swift paid strict attention to expenditure. His surviving account-books reveal his methodical system of costing any journey, but also indicate where such monies were spent, thus providing a sketch-map of his itinerary. Since the journey from Dublin to London usually lasted at least a week, it could become an expensive prelude to the real business in hand. We know that his customary route from Chester was through Whitchurch, Coventry, Towcester, Dunstable and St Albans. The ride from Chester to London usually took about five days, averaging thirty-five miles a day. With meticulous satisfaction, Swift itemised all the significant facts of these travels, sometimes allowing a hint of relish into the record, as in the following entry:

Left Leiceste^r. Mon^d. May 29.
Left Neston. Tues^d. May 30th. 1704
landed at Dublin. Thursday morn.
June 1. 1704. being my 16th Voyage.

That last figure is doubtless prompted by a sense of achievement, a statistical triumph over penitential conditions.

In the summer of 1726, Swift sailed to England, carrying with him a manuscript copy of *Gulliver's Travels*, looking forward to a reunion with friends he had not seen for over ten years. He spent most of that summer with Alexander Pope, at the poet's house in Twickenham on the banks of the Thames, whose elaborate gardens exemplified the latest fashion in "picturesque" landscape. In one of his most elaborate pseudonymous hoaxes, Swift then masqueraded as one "Richard Sympson", cousin of a retired seaman, Lemuel Gulliver, who wished to see his relative's memoirs made available to a reading public who enjoyed tales of remote and exotic places. In a letter to the printer, Benjamin Motte, Sympson emphasised Gulliver's philanthropic motive in publishing the work, saying that "the Author intends the Profit for the use of Poor Seamen". Motte was impressed, and arranged for a speedy publication of this strange story about a ship's surgeon who had seen and experienced so many near-incredible places on the other side of the globe. Not wishing to allow his presence in London to suggest the probable authorship of the *Travels*, Swift returned to Ireland.

No sooner had he arrived back home, than he wrote to Pope, remarking on the strange and fascinating alterations in the cultural landscape which he had observed on his ride north:

> ... you will find what a quick change I made in seven days from London to the Deanery, through many nations and languages unknown to the civilized world. And I have often reflected in how few hours, with a swift horse or a strong gale, a man may come among a people as unknown to him as the Antipodes.

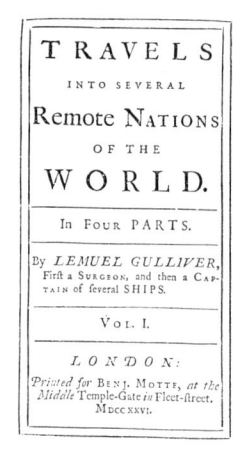

Title-page of first edition of Gulliver's Travels. *(With thanks to Armagh Public Library)*

Gulliver bringing over the fleet of Blefescu to the King of Lilliput, from third "B" edition of Gulliver's Travels *(1726), engraved by C. Du Bosc after J. Grison.*

His imagination full of the unsettling experience of Gulliver, it is as if the author now sees how, even in early eighteenth-century Britain, a similar journey can take place, where the traveller seems to go back in time by rushing forward through space. Once across the Welsh border, the familiar and reassuring culture of Twickenham and Windsor must have seemed like another world, a dream-like era.

The charade which Swift had played with Benjamin Motte backfired badly when it was discovered that the first printed edition of *Gulliver's Travels*, which was published in October 1726, was disfigured by many printing errors. Swift now decided, reluctantly, that he would have to return to London to arrange for an improved, second edition. In April 1727, he set sail from Ireland to oversee negotiations with the printer. This was to be his final voyage to England.

He went from Chester to Herefordshire, to visit his ancestral home in Goodrich, where his paternal grandfather, Thomas, had been vicar during the English Civil War, siding with the

Royalist cause. After this rare sentimental detour, he went straight to London, spending most of the summer with Pope at Twickenham. Swift's authorship of *Gulliver's Travels* was by now the worst-kept secret in the literary world, and his fame had spread across Europe, where French, German and Dutch editions had suddenly appeared. Voltaire, on a visit to England, invited Swift to visit France, assuring him of a welcome and a reception normally reserved for royalty. He even prepared letters of introduction to aristocratic friends, including one to the Comte de Morville, minister and Secretary of State at Versailles. Swift was still very keen to make his first visit to Europe, but his hopes were frustrated, and then abandoned, by the sensational news of the sudden death of King George I on his way to Hanover. Everyone in London, including Swift, waited nervously to see how the monarch's death, and the accession of George II, would affect the political landscape. To the great vexation of many who hoped for a new order, including Swift himself, Walpole's Whig ministry remained in place: Swift's cancellation of his French visit now seemed a wasted and unnecessary caution. Terrible anxiety over reports from Dublin of Stella's fading health intensified his gloom, and he decided to quit London immediately, without even telling Pope, and return home as quickly as possible. On 18 September 1727, along with his manservant Watt, Swift headed north for the last time.

He seems to have made good speed to Chester, reaching this gateway to the coastal ports of Parkgate and Holyhead in four days. He then faced the usual dilemma of which way to turn in order to hasten progress home, whether to ride on for three days to Holyhead and make a shorter crossing by sea, or to ride the few miles to Parkgate and take the longer crossing. It happened that a Captain Lawson was in Chester, commander of the government yacht which lay in Parkgate, and he offered Swift passage to Dublin whenever conditions improved. The Dean

An engraving of Alexander Pope's house at Twickenham, by Peter Rysbrack, c.1735. Note how the guests arrive by the riverside, thus enjoying an unimpeded prospect of this most celebrated, and widely illustrated, landmark of Georgian London. (Courtesy of the Orleans House Gallery, Richmond, Surrey)

declined, and decided to take his chances by pushing on into Wales. His choice of route proved disastrous in personal terms, but resulted in one of the most fully documented episodes in his life-long travels.

Watt and his fifty-nine-year-old master spent their first night at Ridland, then set off early on Saturday morning, passing through Penmaenmawr and Conway, stopping that evening on Anglesey, which they reached by a short ferry from Bangor. At four in the morning, they set off with a guide for Holyhead, which now lay only twenty-two miles away, on the north-western tip of Anglesey. This last stretch proved to be the longest, and most farcical, of the journey. Watt's horse lost two shoes on the rocky terrain, and then Swift's horse in sympathy, lost one of its own. To spare the horses, both men walked, now in desperate need of a smith, not someone easily located on a Sunday. Finally, the sulking guide discovered help, and Swift proceeded to walk to what he called "a hedge Inn", where no ale was available. He secured a small boat from the innkeeper, which took him the last three miles along the coast to Holyhead. When he arrived at the port, like a castaway finally in sight of rescue, he was informed that the boat for Ireland had left on the previous day with a good wind.

Most of the information about Swift's stay at Holyhead on this frightful journey comes from his *Holyhead Journal*, a diary of desperation which he filled every day with a catalogue of frustration. Still preoccupied with the dreadful prospect of Stella dying in his absence, while he sat idle in a Welsh tavern, he addressed the journal to her, thereby creating the small comfort of her imagined company.

Swift and Watt, like characters out of a Beckettian tragicomedy, spent the week getting on each other's nerves, moping around the tavern run by a Mrs Welch, walking among the rocks and caves on the headland, cursing the unintelligibility of the local language. Swift records very disturbing nightmares, including one of repeatedly falling off his horse. He was also running short of clean clothes, but was loath to send Watt in search of a launderer in case he never returned or, worse still, a boat suddenly appeared and the Dean's wardrobe was nowhere to be found. The only feature of the landscape which offered some energetic diversion, as well as a possible view of Ireland, was Holyhead mountain, rising over seven hundred feet, which Swift recalled as Ptolemy's "Sacrum promontorium". The two men climbed the summit (Swift noting, incredibly, that he took breath "59 times") but could not see the Wicklow hills, since "the day was too hazy". On their way down, they had to beat a hasty retreat when overtaken by "a furious shower", finding eventual shelter in "a welch cabin, almost as bad as an Irish one". Cursing everything and everyone, especially Watt, "whose blunders would bear a history", Swift summarised his indignity thus: "In Short: I come from being used like an Emperor to be used worse than a Dog at Holyhead."

In the middle of this forlorn week, a letter arrived from

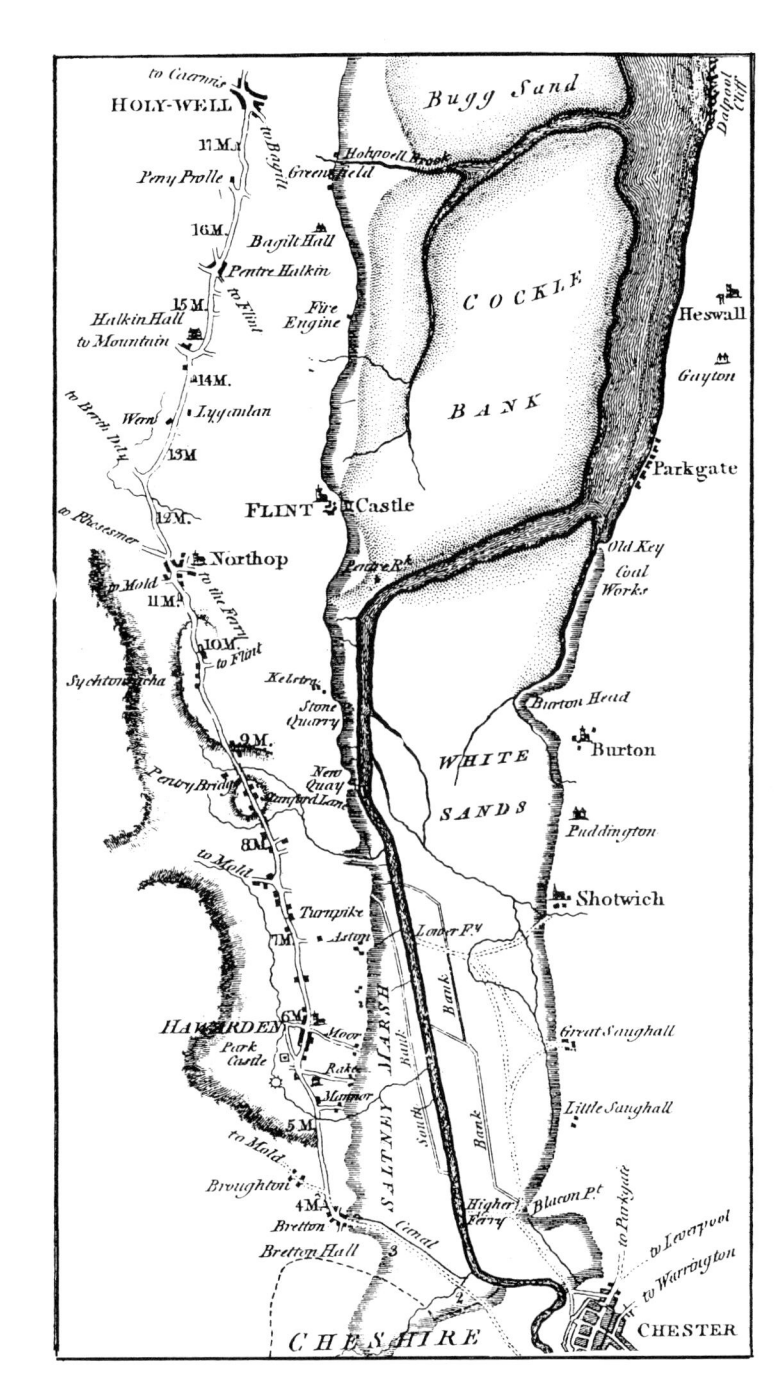

From Actual Survey of the Great Post-Road from London to Parkgate *(1779) by the surveyor Peter Bell. This section shows the crucial crossroad presented by Chester, where the traveller bound for Ireland could stay on the east side of the Dee and head up to Parkgate, or cross the river for the road through Wales. (Courtesy of the National Library of Wales)*

London, signed by a certain John Wheldon (most likely a prankster's pseudonym), whose enquiry had a kind of fantastical appropriateness to the Dean's sense of being stranded between two worlds. Wheldon, addressing Swift as a probable "Lover of the Mathematicks", informed him that he had devised a method for discovering "the Longitude by two known Stars". He tells Swift that he has sent copies of his discourse to various authorities, including the renowned Astronomer Royal, Edmund Halley, and wonders, politely, if the famous Dean could help promote his project. Being hunted down by a crackpot speculator in the wastes of Wales did not amuse Swift, who wrote an impatient, but measured, reply at the bottom of the projector's letter, dismissing the whole thing as a tiresome impertinence, adding, with weary finality, that he was sure Wheldon "would deceive others, or are deceived yourself".

Swift preferred his own kind of ironic speculations, especially those which extracted a grotesque sense of the possible advantages of life in Wales. For those who lamented the all too speedy passage of time, Holyhead was a kind of heaven, a place where "a day is longer than a week, and if the weather be foul, as long as a fortnight". Being nowhere of interest, Holyhead offered the kind of privacy and sanctuary every rational person should desire. Retirement on such a rock, with close friends and a regular supply of good wine was, he imagined, "much better than being a slave in Ireland".

Towards the end of the week, three packets had docked in Holyhead, unable to turn around because of the continuing bad weather. Swift grimly observed a fleet of useless boats, and cursed Aeolus, the temperamental god of the skies. On 28 September, the wind seemed to promise a quick escape, and Swift joined the other hopeful passengers on one of the boats. This false dawn is described by Swift in a subsequent letter to Stella:

> We had not been half an hour in the ship till a fierce wind rose directly against us. We tryed a good while, but the storm still continued: so we turned back, and it was 8 at night, dark and rainy before the ship got back, and at anchor: the other passengers went back in a boat to Holyhead: but to prevent accidents and broken shins I lay all night on board, and came back this morning at 8: am now in my Chamber, where I must stay, and get in a new stock of patience.

As if to show her absolute dominion over these disappointed travellers, Nature suddenly decided to lift the siege, and a boat finally set sail for Dublin over the weekend. One final twist in this testing odyssey remained, however, when the boat was driven by strong winds to shelter in Carlingford Lough, north-east of Dundalk, about sixty miles up the coast from Dublin.

When they finally disembarked, Swift and Watt had to ride for two days to reach home, arriving on 4 October, over two weeks since they had set out from London. The tension and frustration of that fortnight were not due solely to physical inconvenience or discomfort: during that time, Swift's imagination must have been tortured by the possibility of Stella's death. She was still alive when he reached Dublin, but in an irreversible decline. The end was not far off, and she died four months later, aged forty-six, on 28 January 1728. Her death overwhelmed the ageing Dean. On the evening of her death, Swift composed a tribute to her character, describing her as "the truest, most virtuous, and valuable friend, that I, or perhaps any other person ever was blessed with". Stella was laid to rest in the aisle of St Patrick's, where Swift would later join her.

That nightmarish week in Holyhead represented a major turning point in Swift's life, marking the end of his physical contact with England, and the close of his life with Stella. His sense of maddening impotence was shaped into imaginative resistance, however, in a group of five poems, one of which, "Holyhead, 25 September, 1727", rages against the loneliness and the cruelty of the landscape:

> I never was in haste before
> To reach that slavish hateful shore:
> Before, I always found the wind
> To me was most malicious kind,
> But now the danger of a friend
> On whom my hopes and fears depend,
> Absent from whom all climes are cursed,
> With whom I'm happy in the worst,
> With rage impatient makes me wait
> A passage to the land I hate.
> Else, rather on this bleaky shore
> Where loudest winds incessant roar,
> Where neither herb nor tree will thrive,
> Where nature hardly seems alive,
> I'd go in freedom to my grave,
> Than rule yon isle and be a slave.

Swift could appreciate the joke being played by Nature, whereby he was kept out of the country he hated on the sole occasion he passionately wanted to be there. Some of the most powerful emotions of his life – his love for Stella, his entanglement with Ireland, and his voyager's sense of homelessness – are combined in these ironical verses which dramatise his ineffectual struggle to outwit time and circumstance. In many ways, this poem is an epitome of Swift's experience of travel, above all in the sense it gives of the voyager at the mercy of the mysterious, unpredictable and powerful ways of Nature.

A few weeks after his return from Holyhead, and on the eve of his sixtieth birthday, Swift had written a letter to Knightley Chetwode in which his deepening and unrepentant gloom gathered force:

> I wish I had some retirement two or three miles from this town to amuse myself, as you do, with planting much, but not as you do, for I would build very little. But I cannot think of a remote journey in such a miserable country, such a climate, and such roads, and such uncertainty of health. I would never if possible be above an hour distant from home, nor be caught by a deafness and giddiness out of my own precincts, where I can do or not do, what I please; and see or not see, whom I please. But if I had

Stella, by James Latham (1696–1747). (Courtesy of the National Gallery of Ireland)

a home a hundred miles off I never would see this town again, which I believe is the most disagreeable place in Europe, at least to any but those who have been accustomed to it from their youth, and in such a case I suppose a jail might be tolerable. But my best comfort is, that I lead here the life of a monk, as I have always done; I am vexed whenever I hear a knocking at the door, especially the raps of quality, and I see none but those who come on foot.

This complaint is both moving and misleading. It was penned during one of the lowest periods in Swift's emotional life, a winter when some of his most valued forms of friendship were ending. Like Wales, Dublin was both intolerable and strangely suitable, a place of confinement well-adapted to his misanthropic mood.

Yet Swift's powers of recovery always proved stronger than such seemingly conclusive despair, and soon he would be bracing himself for new landscapes and friends, who would restore his need to reassert his imaginative energy and control.

7
Markethill, County Armagh

IN THE summer of 1728, Swift made the first of three successive visits to the estate of Sir Arthur and Lady Acheson, at Markethill, County Armagh. We do not know when he first met the Achesons, but he probably made their acquaintance through mutual friends in Dublin society. Lady Acheson, née Anne Savage, was the daughter of a former Chancellor of the Exchequer for Ireland, Philip Savage, whom Swift had known for nearly twenty years; she was also a close friend of the Rochforts of Gaulstown, probably through Sir Arthur, who was MP for Mullingar, County Westmeath. As Sheriff of County Armagh, Sir Arthur was an important legal figure in the administration. While on official political business in Dublin, he stayed at his Capel Street residence, close to Sheridan's academy.

The Acheson estate lay just a mile north of the small village of Markethill, thirteen miles beyond Newry and only seven miles south-east of Armagh. The seventy-mile route from Dublin to Markethill, passing through Drogheda and Dundalk, would have been familiar to Swift. Acheson himself described this part of County Armagh as a successful colonial settlement:

> . . . the best improved part of Ireland; not inferior to many parts of England; and the fullest of people, and yet a hundred and thirty years ago there was not one British man in all these northern counties. . . . Never surely was any country so much altered in so short a time. We have few or none of the old Irish amongst us; we have indeed plenty of everything but

From Moll's Twenty New and Correct Maps of Ireland *(1728).*

money, which is very much wanted. However, we can live comfortably enough if we are satisfied with our obscurity.

Such a mixed assessment, proud of an industrious conquest, but dismayed by the absent signs of normal prosperity, would have provoked a knowledgeable smile from Swift, someone all too familiar with the contradictory nature of the Irish economy. Markethill was one of those several islands of civility outside of which lay a steadily increasing population with little to do but starve and beg, a human landscape rich in numbers alone.

As was his custom, Swift set off on his summer-expedition in early June. Glad, as always, to be out of Dublin, he nonetheless corresponded regularly with friends in the capital, describing to them how he passed his days, and made repeated requests for personal items to be sent north. He even took the liberty of inviting Sheridan to stay at nearby Hamilton's Bawn, a village two miles north of Markethill, on the road from Armagh to Tandragee. Sheridan, busy with his pupils in Dublin, did not take up the invitation. Swift told his friend that he planned to stay until Christmas, when he would have to return to his cathedral for an official visitation from the archbishop. Apart from that unavoidable responsibility, Swift made clear his determination to remain in the countryside for as long as possible:

> And my Reason of Staying is, to be here the Planting and Pruning Time, &c. I hate *Dublin*, and love the Retirement here, and the Civility of my Hosts.

By the end of the summer, he was asking Sheridan to go across to the Deanery and send up fresh clothes, "a Periwig, and a new riding Gown and Cassock", as well as "a dozen Guineas". What began as a summer interlude had developed into a winter retreat.

Markethill was immortalised by Swift in over a dozen poems which he wrote about the place and his hosts. The Dean seems to have been on much friendlier terms with Lady Acheson than with her retiring husband, and several of the poems allow his hostess the ironic liberty of revealing her secret thoughts about a guest who behaves as if he owns the place, and who seems content to stay forever. Witty and playful, these "Libels", as Swift called them, imagine Lady Acheson's exasperation with her bossy and intrusive guest. In "My Lady's Lamentation", she confides her spleen to the reader:

> Before he came here
> To sponge for good cheer,
> I sat with delight,
> From morning till night. . . .

Now, however, she is forced to comply with Swift's régime for self-improvement, and her days are organised along the lines of a strict and exhausting series of intellectual and physical exercises:

> But, while in an ill tone,
> I murder poor Milton,
> The Dean, you will swear,
> Is at study or prayer.
> He's all the day sauntering,
> With labourers bantering,
> Among his colleagues,
> A Parcel of Teagues,
> (Whom he brings in among us
> And bribes with mundungus).

Swift enjoyed teasing his young hostess by mimicking and then dramatising her indignation with this hyperactive guest whose mania for gardening and building seems to her rather ludicrous in an elderly clergyman. Through such raillery, Swift seems to have strengthened the friendship which the poems themselves call into question. His letters and verses reveal a man in his element, spending his days riding, walking, making "improvements" to the gardens, and playing quadrille with Lady Acheson until the small hours.

Summer-breaks, such as those with the Achesons, offered Swift an opportunity to practice the arts of friendship, but they also gave him the space to write without the daily intrusion of ecclesiastical business. Markethill was one of his most creative

An architectural engraving of Armagh cathedral as it appeared in Swift's day, from The Works of Sir James Ware Concerning Ireland, *by Walter Harris, Dublin, 1739. Named after St Patrick, who founded his principal church on this hill-top site in the fifth century, the cathedral still retained its mediaeval character in the eighteenth century. (It was extensively renovated in the nineteenth century.) Note the Latin dedication to Hugh Boulter, then Archbishop of Armagh, an English appointee detested by Swift.*

retreats, typified by the occasional verses on the place, its environs and its inhabitants. Parallel with this poetical holiday, a series of pamphlets was written (though not always published). Many of these pamphlets dealt with the alarming state of the national economy, and show Swift's imaginative ability to see beyond the demesne walls of Markethill, never allowing himself the illusion that aristocratic culture had no business with such base and unsightly affairs as poverty.

In the spring of 1728, shortly before coming to Markethill, Swift had begun a small weekly paper, *The Intelligencer*, with Thomas Sheridan, in order to stimulate public debate about a range of issues affecting the country, from the state of the arts to projects for promoting agriculture. During the summer, he planned, and later wrote, a fictional appeal from "a Country Gentleman in the North of Ireland", addressed to Swift's Drapier, in which the speaker deplores the forced emigration of so many Ulster Presbyterians to the American colonies, as well as the appalling shortage of money in a stagnant economy.

The gentleman imagines how much worse the general state of affairs must be in the rest of the country than "among us of the *North*, who are esteemed the only thriving People of the Kingdom". Even though Swift detested the Ulster Presbyterians, any drain on the Protestant settlement, especially in the North, threatened the political balance as well as the economic stability of the entire country. Tolerate them he would not, but Swift recognised the strategic importance of the industrious Ulster Scots. This pamphlet was printed in the *The Intelligencer* as No. XIX, in December 1728, and was most probably brought down to Dublin by Swift himself when he attended the official visitation at the cathedral.

The relative prosperity of parts of the North threw into grim perspective the wretchedness of many other parts of the island. In *A Short View of the State of Ireland* (1728), Swift's anonymously published pamphlet, those theorists and apologists who likewise pointed to the entertainments of Dublin society as evidence of the kingdom's stability and prosperity, were singled out as pernicious traitors to truth and common sense. The pamphlet declared, angrily, "There is not one Argument used to prove the Riches of *Ireland,* which is not a logical Demonstration of its Poverty." According to the speaker, Ireland was a nightmarish prospect for curious visitors, who would be overwhelmed, not by the natural beauties of the scenery, but by the horrors of the human landscape. Like a European pariah, the island could not hope to enjoy the flattery of civilised company, since "No strangers from other Countries, make this a Part of their Travels; where they can expect to see nothing, but Scenes of Misery and Desolation." No sane person would make Ireland part of a grand European tour, since the place offended every moral and aesthetic grace. The *Short View* was reprinted in *The Intelligencer* in the following year. The pattern of Swift's writing during this period shows both single-mindedness and adaptability: he would let nothing interfere with his precious jaunts into the countryside but, at the same time, would not allow this kind of withdrawal to deflect him from his responsibilities as a public-spirited writer.

Swift's first visit to Markethill lasted nine months, until February 1729, when he finally returned to Dublin. In a letter to Pope, he reflected on this unusually long stay with new friends:

> I lived very easily in the country: Sir Acheson is a man of Sense, and a scholar, has a good voice, and my Lady a better; she is perfectly well bred, and desirous to improve her understanding, which is very good, but cultivated too much like a fine Lady. She was my pupil there, and severely chid when she read wrong; with that, and walking and making twenty little amusing improvements, and writing family verses of mirth by way of libels on my Lady, my time past very well and in very great order. . . .

Recalling the hospitality and friendship which he enjoyed on this first visit, Swift urged Pope to spend a holiday in Dublin, promising him the same rewards for his efforts. Characterising himself as a man happily retired from public controversies, he defended Dublin as a more intimate city than London, and tried to lure his friend across the Irish Sea with assurances of plentiful wine and cider, the best of civil company, sessions of backgammon every Sunday evening, and an invigorating climate which would improve anybody's ill-health. Despite Swift's enthusiastic and repeated invitations, Pope never set foot in Ireland: the friendship between the two most famous writers of their age was preserved, at a distance, through the regular exchange of letters.

Only four months after returning from his first visit to Markethill, Swift headed north yet again and lodged with the Achesons from June until October. In early August, he wrote to Pope about the state of his health, which had improved reasonably well, thanks to the country air, and compared his condition to that of a horse "which though off his mettle, can trot on tolerably". The state of the nation, however, seemed chronically, terminally corrupt, a spectacle which darkened much of what Swift wrote during this period:

> As to this country, there have been three terrible years dearth of corn, and every place strowed with beggars, but dearths are common in better climates, and our evils here lie much deeper. Imagine a nation the two-thirds of whose revenues are spent out of it, and who are not permitted to trade with the other third, and where the pride of the women will not suffer them to wear their own manufactures even where they excel what come from abroad: this is the true state of Ireland in a very few words. These evils operate more every day, and the kingdom is absolutely undone, as I have been telling it often in print these ten years past.

Even though, in this same letter, he could refer to himself as "a stranger in a strange land", Swift's observations about the country and its inhabitants are always fired by outraged devotion. Politically and financially, Swift was committed to the prospect of a stable and improving Ireland: culturally and socially, he was always most at home within Protestant Ireland. His mannered aloofness, his frequent contempt, are sometimes expressed for the benefit of outsiders, but are also, more profoundly, ways of distancing emotion in the interests of an orderly passion.

Swift's principled commitment and critical loyalty to Ireland found regular, practical opportunities for self-expression, none more welcome than the chance to build and develop property. During the summer of 1729, he announced his intention to build a summer residence near Markethill, in the townland of Drumlack, just west of the road to Portadown. At the end of August, this declaration appeared in poetic form as "Drapier's Hill" in London's *Fog's Weekly Journal*. To announce his retirement to Drumlack as a major social event in the cosmopolitan calendar was Swift's way of elevating an Irish townland to the dignified level of famous English homes distinguished by their aristocratic hospitality. It also reflected an irresistible parodic urge to subvert certain classics of this topographical genre, such as Ben Jonson's "To Penshurst" (1612) and Sir John Denham's "Cooper's Hill" (1642). In "Drapier's Hill", Swift explains that he will buy the land from Sir Arthur who, in turn, will name the projected house after Ireland's most renowned patriot:

> That when the nation long enslaved,
> Forgets by whom it once was saved;
> When none the Drapier's praise shall sing;
> His signs aloft no longer swing;
> His medals and his prints forgotten,
> And all his handkerchiefs are rotten;
> His famous *Letters* made waste paper;
> This hill may keep the name of Drapier:
> In spite of envy flourish still,
> And Drapier's vie with Cooper's Hill.

One of many poems in which Swift enjoyed speculating about his posthumous reputation, "Drapier's Hill" proclaims its faith in property rather than poetry, in a monument to taste rather than in the productions of taste themselves.

As intended, the poem was spotted by several of Swift's friends in London. Pope wrote to Markethill, expressing his delight that "Drapier's Hill is to emulate Parnassus", adding, "I fear the country about it is as much impoverished." Three weeks later, however, he received a reply from Swift, then back in Dublin, in which the Dean explained that he had abandoned the entire project:

> ... I will fly as soon as build; I have neither years, nor spirits, nor money, nor patience for such amusements. The frolick is gone off, and I am only 100l the poorer. But this kingdom is grown so excessively poor, that we wise men must think of nothing but getting a little ready money. It is thought there are not two hundred thousand pounds of species in the whole island; for we return thrice as much to our Absentees, as we get by trade, and so are all inevitably undone; which I have been telling them in print these ten Years, to as little purpose as if it came from the pulpit.

Swift's disgruntled manner here, dismissing a project which only a few months earlier had excited him, conceals a personal hurt expressed in a poem, "The Dean's Reasons for not Building at Drapier's Hill", written after this second visit but never published in his lifetime. In this poem, Swift portrays Sir Arthur as an unfriendly host whose "uncommunicative heart" shuns all approaches and proposals from his guest who, in turn, is angered by the slight to his own person. Swift declares that the house and grounds are wasted on such an anti-social recluse, and gladly forecasts ruin and revenge on such a misanthrope. Swift's attention and dedication to Lady Acheson may also have accounted for the sudden reserve between the two men.

Swift's personal disenchantment with Sir Arthur in that summer of 1729 coincides with a more impersonal, and much more savage, rejection, namely, that of any hope of reforming Ireland. During these months, he composed his most radical pamphlet on Irish affairs and, simultaneously, on the art of pamphleteering itself. In *A Modest Proposal* he imitated the seductive reasoning of projectors (like himself) who promised radical solutions to national crises, and who delighted in elaborate and detailed illustration of their methods. The anonymous speaker in the pamphlet proposes the cannibalism of children as an effective and profitable solution to national poverty and

Blamount was the home of the Black family, Belfast wine-merchants, who purchased the estate in 1757. Also known as Ballinteggart House, it lies between Portadown and Loughgall. It is likely that the Blacks invented this illustrious connection with their new home, a place never mentioned by Swift. Some local historians believe that it actually represents Markethill, which lies eighteen miles to the south. (Courtesy of the National Library of Ireland)

unemployment. If, as theorists suggest, people are the true riches of a nation, then, argues Swift's projector, the useless, starving hordes of children should be turned into an economic and edible asset. With ironic relish, Swift satirises the vanity of philanthropic writers, as well as the hypocrisy of those who object to the scheme out of some long-disused Christian scruple. The projector behind *A Modest Proposal* deliberately scandalises his readers, and leaves them in painful moral confusion. He even lists countless schemes proposed over the previous decade by Swift himself, and dismisses them with triumphant disdain:

> . . . let no Man talk to me of these and the like Expedients; till he hath, at least, a Glimpse of Hope, that there will ever be some hearty and sincere Attempt to put *them in Practice*.

The humour behind *A Modest Proposal* is grim indeed, nurtured by a violent exasperation with idle and deceptive talk, and now happy to show its audience the physical logic of treating people like animals.

As we have seen, especially in the correspondence with Pope, the calamitous state of the country, as well as a sense of the futility of writing about it, preoccupied Swift during that summer. Such despondence influenced the design and tone of *A Modest Proposal*, the darkest pamphlet he ever wrote. He drafted and corrected it at Markethill during the autumn, and then brought it down to Dublin in early October. According to a contemporary report in the *Dublin Intelligencer*, he "was received with great joy by many of our principal citizens, who also on the same occasion caused the bells to ring in our cathedrals, and had bonfires and other illuminations". The pamphlet was printed and published at the end of October by Sarah Harding, widow of John Harding, printer of *The Drapier's Letters*. It was a great commercial success, being reprinted in a variety of Dublin and London editions within months of its original appearance. An outrageous triumph, this marked the end of Swift's passionate involvement with Irish national affairs: he wrote only a few, rather predictable, pamphlets on religious and municipal affairs after 1730, and turned away from those controversies which had dominated his attention since becoming Dean of St Patrick's.

During the winter of 1729, Swift contented himself at the Deanery with social evenings, limited exercise and his daily correspondence. He told Pope that his health was mending, "being cured of Irish politicks by despair". In early 1730, he wrote to his old friend in London, John Gay, author of *The Beggar's Opera* (1728), describing his energetic personal routine: "I ride and walk whenever good Weather invites, and am reputed the best Walker in this Town and five Miles around." He wrote to Bolingbroke in the spring, complaining of the tedious morbidity of an ageing mind, but remarked, in happy contradiction, "I love *la bagatelle* better than ever." In May, sounding eminently sensible, he wrote to Pope:

> ... yet I hitherto walk as much, and ride oftner than formerly. I intend to make no distant journey this Summer even here, nor be above two nights out of the power of returning to my home.

In the following month he was back at Markethill, ignoring his own caution. Having written, but not published, his poem about Sir Arthur's grudging company, it seems astonishing that he would have returned for more discourtesy from someone he had ceased to respect or even tolerate. There must have been enough promise of time to be enjoyed with Lady Acheson to convince him of the value and benefit of the journey.

During a very active summer at Markethill, Swift composed a poetical tribute to Lady Acheson's good taste in friends, in which she sings the praises and extols the talents of her clerical guest. As a piece of ironic flattery, "A Panegyric on the Dean" gives us a witty self-portrait of someone who delights, and surprises, his hostess with his many practical arts:

You merit new employments daily:
Our thatcher, ditcher, gardener, bailie,
And, to a genius so extensive,
No work is grievous or offensive.
Whether, your fruitful fancy lies
To make for pigs convenient sties:
Or, ponder long with anxious thought,
To banish rats that haunt our vault.
Nor have you grumbled, reverend Dean,
To keep our poultry sweet and clean;
To sweep the mansion house they dwell in;
And cure the rank unsavoury smelling.

In keeping with this industrious rhythm, the Dean's architectural legacy to the estate at Markethill is then revealed as two outdoor privies, dedicated to the "gentle goddess Cloacine", twin artefacts of the civilising urge. This "Panegyric" develops into one of the many scatological poems written by Swift to mock the absurdly idealised versions of the female imagination, and to demonstrate a more realistic sensibility than the conventions of decorum permit. At the risk of seeming to indulge a taste for obscenity, Swift pays Lady Acheson the extreme compliment of being a frank and natural woman in a culture which normally represses such virtues.

This poem was Swift's valediction to the pleasures of Markethill. Despite the awkwardness with her husband, Swift enjoyed the hospitality, conviviality and freedom of the place, a setting and a company which inspired his poetic wit as few other places did. As if in sympathy with Swift's sense of distance, Lady Acheson soon separated from her husband, and went to live with her mother at the Grange, near Baldoyle, on the north side of Dublin, from where she remained in touch with the Dean until her death in 1737.

In 1776, the Acheson's son, Archibald, became the first Viscount Gosford on his elevation to the peerage. In that same year, Arthur Young, the celebrated agriculturalist and traveller, visited the new viscount at his estate, as part of a fact-finding

Gosford Castle, Markethill, County Armagh.

tour of the island. Although half a century separates Young's passing visit from Swift's time there, a familiar confusion of industry and backwardness still seemed to distinguish the area:

> Take the road to Markethill. I am now got into the linen country, and the worst husbandry I have met with. . . . All the farms are very small, let to weavers, etc. This road is abominably bad, continually over hills, rough, stony, and cut up. It is a turnpike, which in Ireland is a synonymous term for a vile road; which is the more extraordinary, as the bye ones are the finest in the world.

Young noted that the religion in the area was "mostly Roman", but that manufacturers were "generally Protestant". The linen industry of the North, which Swift had envied and praised, continued to thrive into the nineteenth century.

In 1819, the mansion in which the Achesons had received Swift was torn down; the first example of Norman-revival in Ireland, Gosford Castle, was built in its place. In 1958 the entire estate, comprising some two hundred and forty hectares, was sold to the Forestry Service, and since then has been designated as a conservation area. Gosford Castle still stands, and the walled-gardens which Swift helped to design and cultivate are open to the public.

8
Final Journeys

DURING the last decade of his literary and clerical career, Swift continued to show extraordinary and defiant resourcefulness, especially in the ways he began to organise the writings of a lifetime. Knowing that publishers in both Dublin and London were very keen to secure rights over his work, and that manuscripts of unpublished writings were scattered throughout Ireland and England (often in the homes of friends and correspondents), he was anxious to retain as much personal control as possible over his legacy and reputation. This determination required diplomatic, often deceptive, negotiations and arrangements with friends and publishers.

Alexander Pope was one of those most keen to celebrate their friendship and achievement in new, definitive editions of their writings, and began to assemble materials for that purpose. In his replies to Pope's regular entreaties for manuscripts, Swift usually painted a self-portrait of one who was world-weary, an old man who had retired from the world of letters. In January 1731, he wrote to Pope:

> I dine tête à tête five times a week with my old Presbyterian Housekeeper, whom I call Sir Robert, and so do all my friends & Neighbours. I am in my Chamber at five, there sit alone till eleven, and then to bed. I write Pamphlets and follys meerly for amusement, and when they are finished, as I grow weary in the middle, I cast them into the fire, partly out of dislike, and chiefly because I know they will signify nothing. I walk much every day and ride once or twice a week and so you have the whole State of my life.

This image of an eccentric hermit is largely a seasonal version of an existence which was still very active socially, partly a delaying tactic to give himself more time to consider the best possible direction for his literary estate. His repeated indifference to literary reputation is both principled and strategic, a statement about a career based on public service rather than self-interest, and a decoy to confuse the competition.

During these final years, there are regular examples of Swift privately working against time and ill-health in order to collect his unfinished work into definitive form. In the summer of 1731, for example, he went down to Powerscourt, County Wicklow, at the invitation of Rev. John Towers, where he tried to finish work on two major projects. These came to be known as *A Complete Collection of Genteel and Ingenious Conversation*, a satirical work, in dramatic form, on the witless style of aristocratic speech, and *Directions to Servants*, a manual of advice, often ironic, on what a master may expect from those whose duty it is to make life bearable for him. Swift had been collecting material for these lengthy pieces for over twenty years, and was now using his summer holidays away from the demands of the Deanery to revise these elaborate works. The *Ingenious Conversation* was published in 1738, while *Directions to Servants* was not published until 1745, the year of Swift's death. Both publications reflect Swift's concern with social decorum, especially its speech, and note its abuse and neglect by the upper and lower classes, those who promoted, and those who served, the cause of civilised society.

A satirist usually believes in the redemptive or curative power of his art. While England continued to represent Swift's original model of a civil nation, one whose abuses could be corrected

Ferries were a vital mode of transport in Swift's age. This list, from Moll's Twenty New and Correct Maps of Ireland (1728), identifies twenty-six crossings, important information for the traveller, especially in the absence of safe and reliable bridges.

and improved through exposure, Ireland frustrated all such faith. By the 1730s, however, such an unyielding contrast began to assume a more complex and questionable character, a shift brought about by long absence from England and long endurance in Ireland. Seeing himself as an authority on both countries, bound to one, devoted to the other, Swift sometimes enjoyed lecturing English visitors on the incomparable horrors of Ireland. In the summer of 1732, he wrote to John Brandreth, rector of Knocktopher, County Kilkenny, and newly appointed Dean of Armagh. (Brandreth had been granted the prestigious Deanery by the Duke of Dorset, whose eldest son he had tutored.) Emphasising his familiarity with Kilkenny, Swift declared the place to be typical of the country as a whole:

> ... a bare face of nature, without houses or plantations; filthy cabins, miserable, tattered, half-starved creatures, scarce in human shape; one insolent ignorant oppressive squire to be found in twenty miles riding; a parish church to be found only in a summer day's journey, in comparison of which, an English farmer's barn is a cathedral; a bog of fifteen miles round; every meadow a slough, and every hill a mixture of rock, heath, and marsh; and every male and female, from the farmer, inclusive to the day-labourer, infallibly a thief, and consequently a beggar, which in this island are terms convertible.

One cannot help feeling that such a relentless litany of barbarism is partly motivated by a malicious pleasure in watching an English innocent step into the mire of a corrupt colony. On the other hand, Swift may well wish to disassociate himself from such a scene through an appeal to a supposedly shared sense of superiority towards such backwardness. Ultimate political responsibility for the waste and calamity, however, is not in question, and Swift tells Brandreth, bluntly, that "all these evils are effects of English tyranny". Swift's explanation of Ireland's disorder is sometimes that of the sneering colonist, who attributes all misery to the innate sloth of the natives, sometimes that of the disillusioned loyalist, who sees only betrayal. In his later years, it was the conviction based on experience, rather than the prejudice fuelled by background, which directed his observations about Ireland.

This changing sense of defensive loyalty to Ireland is given unequivocal and warm expression in a most unusual letter which Swift wrote to Charles Wogan, in August 1732, where he makes clear how experience and observation have altered his earlier antipathy towards the native Irish. Wogan was a Jacobite exile from a distinguished Galway family, a soldier who had served with the Irish regiment in France, had helped in the rescue of Clementina Sobieski from Innsbruck that she might marry the Old Pretender, and was now in service with the Spanish army. Having heard of Swift's reputation as a champion of Irish liberty, he had sent him a packet of miscellaneous writings of his own for the Dean to criticise and correct. In his lengthy and considered reply, Swift first congratulated Wogan on his learning and eloquence – qualities, he noted, rarely found in the military profession and almost never associated with the Irish nation. For the first time in his life, Swift found himself addressing a native aristocrat:

> ... I cannot but highly esteem those Gentlemen of *Ireland*, who, with all the Disadvantages of being Exiles and Strangers, have been able to distinguish themselves by their Valour and Conduct in so many Parts of *Europe*, I think above all other Nations, which ought to make the *English* ashamed of the Reproaches they cast on the Ignorance, the Dulness, and the want of Courage, in the *Irish* Natives; those Defects, wherever they happen, arising only from the Poverty and Slavery they suffer from their inhuman Neighbours, and the base corrupt Spirits of too many of the chief Gentry. . . .

In this liberal absolution of the native Irish from blame for their sorry condition, Swift goes on to substantiate his defence of the victims of oppression by telling Wogan of his years of experience of everyday Irish realities:

> I do assert that from several Experiments I have made in travelling over both Kingdoms, I have found the poor Cottagers here, who could speak

our Language, to have much better natural Taste for good Sense, Humour, and Raillery, than ever I observed among People of the like Sort in *England*. But the Millions of Oppressions they lye under, the Tyranny of their Landlords, the ridiculous Zeal of their Priests, and the general Misery of the whole Nation, have been enough to damp the best Spirits under the Sun.

Behind this rare tribute to the native character is Swift's eager sympathy for, and ready identification with, a fellow-exile. Wogan's Jacobitism is never once mentioned: more important to Swift is the compliment paid to him by a man of honour and learning, someone whose travels around Europe reveal a principled form of exile. Wogan was an unimaginable character to the imperial mind, but for Swift he was happy proof of English ignorance.

While Pope continued to appeal to his friend for manuscripts to be sent to him, Swift was privately negotiating with George Faulkner, whom he later called the "Prince of Dublin Printers", to bring out the first edition of his complete works, repeatedly assuring Pope that such a scheme was against his will and beyond his control. Having given up all hope of a visit to England, he concentrated on what he knew would be his final literary efforts. In the years 1732 and 1733, he wrote several polemical pamphlets attacking moves by London to repeal the Test Act, which excluded Presbyterians from holding public office. His influence in such debates was still crucial and respected: after a short and bitter contest, the Irish parliament rejected any change towards toleration. Swift was a life-long supporter of the Penal Laws, and regarded Presbyterians as a more dangerous, because a more closely related, enemy than Roman Catholics.

Swift conducted most of these campaigns from his study in the Deanery, and rarely felt well enough to venture far outside the city. He tried, yet again, to entice Pope over to Dublin, proclaiming its natural and social advantages:

The conveniences of taking the Air, Winter or Summer, do so far exceed those in London, For the two large Strands just at two edges of the town are as firm & dry in Winter, as in Summer. There are at least six or eight gentlemen of sience, Learning good humour & tast, able & desirous to please you, and orderly females, some of the better sort, to take care of you.

No longer fit for sea-travel, Swift explains his contentment with his little empire:

> ... I walk the streets in peace, without being justled, nor ever without a thousand blessings from my friends the Vulgar. I am Lord Mayor of 120 houses, I am absolute Lord of the greatest Cathedral in the Kingdom: am at Peace with the neighbouring Princes, the Lord Mayor of the City, and the A. Bp. of Dublin. ...

When he chose to be sociable, Swift usually visited friends who lived on the outskirts of the city, such as Dr Patrick Delany and his wife Mary, at Delville, near Glasnevin, only a few miles from the Deanery. The company often included Thomas Sheridan, the writers Laetitia Pilkington and Mary Barber, Dr Helsham, Fellow of Trinity College, and John Boyle, Earl of Orrery. Swift

A prospect of the Custom House and Essex Bridge, by Joseph Tudor, one of a set of six pictures of Dublin published in 1753 in London. This picture gives a dramatic sense of how central the River Liffey was to the social traffic of the city, with quite large ships now able to sail right up to the Custom House, and parties of gentlemen (bottom left) preferring to row, rather than walk or ride, around the city. The equestrian statue on Essex Bridge is of George I. (Courtesy of the National Library of Ireland)

Howth House, by Francis Wheatley, London, 1831. (Courtesy of the National Library of Ireland)

told Ford that, when the weather permitted, he would ride out as far as Howth Castle, where he was entertained by Lord and Lady Howth, neighbours of Lady Acheson at Baldoyle and the Grattans of Belcamp. On one of these visits to Howth, in the summer of 1735, Swift sat to have his portrait executed by Francis Bindon, amateur painter and architect from County Clare. This painting, the first of several by Bindon, still hangs in Howth Castle.

Economy was one of the many resultant virtues of Swift's narrower field of travel. In his late sixties, the Dean was careful to control his income, derived mainly from tithes, in order to preserve a comfortable standard of living for himself, to ensure that his retinue of household servants remained with him at all times of need, and to protect those savings which he planned to donate to some public charity. As he explained in a letter to John Arbuthnot, an old friend from his time with the Tories, and former Royal Physician, the expense as much as the discomfort of long journeys precluded any thoughts of a final reunion in London:

> I have here a large convenient house; I live at two thirds cheaper than I could there, I drink a bottle of French wine my self every day, though I love it not; but it is the onely thing that keeps me out of pain, I ride every fair day a dozen miles, on a large Strand, or Turnpike roads; You in London have no such Advantages.... When I ride to a friend a few miles off, if he be not richer than I, I carry My Bottle, my Bread and Chicken, that he may be no loser; I talk thus foolishly to let you know the reasons which joyned to my ill health make it impossible for me to see you and my other friends.

Free of the anxiety, as well as the lure, of a trip to England, Swift contented himself with the simplicity and independence of his life around Dublin, a place which suddenly appeared to offer endless advantages to a man who had spent so many of his earlier years escaping from its confines.

Swift's love of visiting friends was now increasingly threatened by his dread of falling ill *en route*, and being unable to return safely to the Deanery. On several occasions he was forced to abandon plans for an outing, or to decline an invitation to stay in the country, because he no longer trusted his health to carry him to his destination. One such reluctant refusal was to William Richardson, MP for Coleraine and secretary to the Derry Society, the northern trading company. Swift pointed out in his reply that he knew the northern roads very well, adding that County Armagh "is the best part I have seen of Ireland". In early December 1734, he wrote to Rev. John Blachford, at Murrow, near Kilcoole, County Wicklow, inviting himself to spend Christmas and the New Year with the clergyman's family. A week later he wrote again, saying that he could no longer contemplate such a visit. He explained that, on a ride out to Howth on the previous day, he had suffered "a fit of that giddyness which at times hath pursued me from my youth", and had been forced to seek shelter and rest in an empty house on the road for several hours. Such unpredictable attacks terrified Swift.

In the spring of 1735, Theophilus Bolton, now Archbishop of Cashel, wrote to Swift inviting him to spend a fortnight of the summer with him. Knowing the Dean's enthusiasm for all projects to improve clerical livings, Bolton outlined his plans to spend £1,000 on repairs to the cathedral, and suggested that Swift give his advice on the design drawn up for the restoration. He also recommended the sublime beauty of the place itself, especially King Cormac's chapel, an outstanding example of Irish Romanesque dating from the twelfth century.

Swift regretfully declined the invitation, saying that old-age and ill-health made such a journey unthinkable. Bolton, however, repeated his entreaty, detailing the most convenient route from Dublin, and offering to assist the Dean over the last leg of the journey:

> I am truly concerned at the account you give me of y^r health; without doubt a southern ramble will prove the best remedy you can take to recover y^r flesh; and I don't know, except in one stage, where you can chuse a road so suited to y^r circumstances, as from Dublin hither – you have to Kilkenny a turnpike and good inns at every ten or twelve miles end. from Kilkenny hither is twenty long miles bad road, and no inn at all; But I have an expedient for that; at the foot of a very high hill just midway there lives in a neat thatcht Cabbin, a Parson who is not poor, his wife is allowed to be the best little Woman in the world, her chickens are the fattest and her ale the best in all the County.

Bolton was referring to Rev. John Walsh, who lived at Fennor, the corps of a prebend in Cashel Cathedral. Doing his utmost to relieve Swift of any fear of hardship or abandonment, he offered to meet his friend at Fennor, where they could rest overnight, and continue the last stage of the road to Cashel in Bolton's private coach.

Swift never made this trip, despite Bolton's reassurances of assistance and accommodation. On this occasion, as so often before, ill-health was only one reason for not leaving Dublin. For several

The Rock of Cashel, County Tipperary, from Antiquities of Ireland, *by Francis Grose, London, 1791–95.*

months now, Swift had been quietly helping George Faulkner in the preparation of an authoritative edition of his writings. The first four volumes of Swift's *Works* were published by January 1735, introducing an edition which was finally complete in 1769, consisting of twenty octavo volumes. He was also preoccupied with drafting a lengthy and detailed will and testament. In the summer of 1735, he wrote to Lord Orrery:

> I have been some months settling my perplexed affairs, like a dying man, and like the dying man pestred with continuall Interruptions as well as difficultyes. I have now finished my will in form, wherein I have settled my whole Fortune on the City, in trust for building and maintaining an Hospital for Idiots and Lunaticks. . . .

This central feature of his final wishes resulted in the foundation, in 1746, of St Patrick's Hospital, Ireland's and Europe's first psychiatric asylum.

When Theophilus Bolton died, in 1744, he also made a bequest of enduring value to the nation. This was his extensive antiquarian library (which then included several thousand volumes from the personal library of Archbishop King, who had died in 1729), donated *in perpetuo* to the Archbishop and clergy of the diocese of Cashel. Rehoused in the grounds of St John the Baptist Cathedral in the nineteenth century, the library was eventually restored and officially reopened in 1986. Now renamed the GPA-Bolton Library, it holds one of Ireland's most important collections of antiquarian literature.

Reflections on Swift's age and infirmity occur in nearly every letter which he wrote during this period, as in one to Lord Oxford, in September 1735, where he seems to resign himself to enforced isolation in the Deanery, concluding, "I can not now bear the common hardships of travelling". Incredibly, even while writing such sentiments to people like Oxford about his stoical incapacity, he was bracing himself for one final and exhausting expedition.

At the end of September 1735, Swift wrote to Sheridan, hinting at an escape from Dublin while the new parliamentary session, to be opened by the Duke of Dorset, was underway. The Irish parliament now sat in a splendid new building in College Green, opened in 1732, designed by Edward Lovett Pearce, MP for Ratoath, County Meath, who was also responsible for the magnificent new library at Trinity College. Swift disliked the pomp and ceremony associated with the opening of parliament, especially the tiring social rounds which followed, and held the members of that body in very low esteem, telling Sheridan, " I am not able to live within the Air of such Rascals."

Sheridan, now teaching at the Royal School in Cavan town, was delighted at the prospect of a reunion, and replied immediately, suggesting the best route from Dublin to Cavan, and telling Swift that he would meet him at Virginia, where they would stop overnight, continuing the fifteen miles to Cavan the next day.

The Dean set off on 3 November, now wearing gambadoes, long riding-boots attached to the saddle to ease the pain and discomfort of such journeys. Three days after he arrived, he wrote a joint letter with his host to Mrs Whiteway in Dublin, a cousin who was now acting as his housekeeper and guardian, detailing the stages of his arduous ride north:

> Nov. 3, to *Dunshallan*, twelve long miles, very weary; Nov. 4, to *Kells*, sixteen miles, ten times wearier; the 5th, to *Cross keys*, seventeen long miles, fifty times wearier; the 6th, to *Cavan*, five miles, weariest of all: Yet I baited every day, And dined where I lay; and this very day I am weary, and my shin bad, yet I never looked on it. I have been now the third day at *Cavan*, the Doctor's *Canaan*, the dirtiest place I ever saw, with the worst wife and daughter, and the most cursed sluts and servants on this side *Scotland*.

This gloomy manner was partly intended to provoke his writing-partner into a defence of the joys of Cavan, something which Sheridan proceeded to outline to Mrs Whiteway, thus setting up a playful epistolary banter between the two clerics.

From subsequent letters, all written in the same form of comic dialogue, we learn a great deal about how the two men entertained themselves. They quickly ran out of drink, and Swift wrote to Mrs Whiteway asking her to contact his personal wine-merchant, a Mr Shiell, and order him to send up "twelve dozen of wine in bottles ready packt up". Swift complained regularly

A prospect of the new Parliament House, by Joseph Tudor, London, 1753. The perspective looks up towards Dame Street (where Tudor, a Dublin painter, lived), giving us a glimpse of fashionable society moving around a district well-served with sedan-chairs. (Courtesy of the National Library of Ireland)

about his health and the weather, more out of habit than conviction, yet he enjoyed describing to Mrs Whiteway the abundance of fresh food, especially wildfowl, remarking, "It is nothing to have a present of a dozen snipes, teal, woodcock, widgeon, duck, and mallard." Local dignitaries regularly called upon the famous Dean who, in turn, invited sixteen of "the principal men in town" to dine with him at the best tavern in the town. Sheridan assured Mrs Whiteway "that the Dean begins to look healthier and plumper already", and made ironic complaint of the cost of entertaining such an appetite. Swift celebrated his sixty-eighth birthday on 30 November, and Mrs Whiteway informed him that his friends in Dublin had toasted the health of the Drapier that evening, and that the bells of his cathedral had been rung in his honour.

Swift came back to Dublin for Christmas, and started work on a lengthy satirical poem inspired by that assembly of politicians which had earlier persuaded him to flee the city. When he heard that the Irish MPs were voting on legislation to deprive the Established Church of many of its tithes, and were doing so in a monument to their own vanity, he took witty and scathing poetical revenge on such venality. Comparing the MPs to the diabolical inhabitants of the underworld, he composed *A Character, Panegyric, and Description of the Legion Club*, which opens with observations upon the symbolic incongruity of Pearce's new building being so close to centres of learning and religion, Trinity College and St Andrew's Round Church:

> As I stroll the city, oft I
> Spy a building large and lofty,
> Not a bow-shot from the College,
> Half a globe from sense and knowledge.
> By the prudent architect
> Placed against the church direct;
> Making good my grandam's jest,
> *Near the church* – you know the rest.

Dublin Castle, a view of the upper Castle Court, by Joseph Tudor, London, 1753. (Courtesy of the National Library of Ireland)

Because the poem went on to vilify certain politicians by name, Swift decided it would be safer to have the work published anonymously in London, although he seems to have allowed copies to circulate in Dublin, where it was not printed officially until after his death. Nothing enraged Swift so passionately as the spectacle of the State trying to rob the Church, a kind of betrayal which confirmed his despair and loathing for the Irish administration.

Even when Ireland tried to honour Swift, her agents seemed to do so in ways that confirmed his distrust of most public figures. In March 1737, Lord Orrery, on business in Cork, wrote to tell Swift that the aldermen of that city had agreed to honour the ageing Dean with the freedom of Cork. It had been arranged that Eaton Stannard, MP for Midleton in that county, and Recorder of Dublin, would present Swift with a silver box to mark the occasion. The box was duly delivered, bearing neither the name of the donor, nor any citation to the recipient. Faced, once again, with a blank memorial, Swift returned the gift, enclosing a sarcastic letter to the Mayor of Cork, Thomas Farren, asking him:

> . . . to insert the Reasons for which you were pleased to give me my Freedom, or bestow the Box upon some more worthy Person, whom you may have an Intention to Honour, because it will equally fit every Body.

The offending box was quickly inscribed, and sent back up to Dublin. Unlike the golden box which he had received from Dublin, seven years previously, this container did not excite Swift's affections, and was left in his will to John Grattan, suggesting that it best be used for holding his favourite tobacco.

Knowing that he would not have long to live, Swift drew upon his formidable, surviving energies to arrange circumstances attendant upon his death. In January 1738, he wrote to John Barber, former Lord Mayor of London:

> I have not been out of Doors further than my Garden, for severall Months, and unless the Summer will assist me, I believe there will be the end of My Travells.

He then arranged for the publication, in London and Dublin, of what has come to be regarded as one of his most outstanding and cryptic poems, *Verses on the Death of Dr. Swift*, in which he imagines the posthumous gossip and debate which his departure will generate. After dramatising the relief and envy felt by many, Swift gives expression to the voice of a solitary, anonymous individual loyal to the Dean's memory:

> 'He gave the little wealth he had,
> To build a house for fools and mad:
> And showed by one satiric touch,
> No nation wanted it so much:
> That kingdom he hath left his debtor,
> I wish it soon may have a better.'

In the summer of 1740, a year after the *Verses* had appeared, Swift wrote one of his last notes, to Mrs Whiteway, in which he confessed to being "so stupid and confounded, that I cannot express the mortification I am under both in body and mind". He had just completed a final draft of his will, and urged her to notify all his nine executors to be ready for his imminent death. He survived, silently, for five more years, and passed away on 19 October 1745, aged seventy-eight.

The last portrait of Swift, painted around 1740 when he was seventy-three. The artist is unknown, but it is quite likely to have been Francis Bindon, for whom Swift had already sat on several occasions. A sign of Swift's withdrawal from society is the absence of his customary periwig, and its replacement by a simple skull-cap. This is the most realistic of all the portraits of Swift. (Courtesy of the National Gallery of Ireland)

Epilogue

In his will, Swift included precise instructions about being interred in the aisle of St Patrick's Cathedral. He had even prepared his own epitaph, written in Latin, which welcomed death as a relief from rage, and which proclaimed a living faith in the righteousness of his art.

W. B. Yeats translated the epitaph into a verse of his own, keeping very closely to the original sense and meaning, but modifying the central image in a way which suggests that the most inspiring, the most moral, adventures are those which take place in the imagination:

> Swift has sailed into his rest;
> Savage indignation there
> Cannot lacerate his breast.
> Imitate him if you dare,
> World-besotted traveller; he
> Served human liberty.

Bibliography

Swift's Writings

The Prose Works of Jonathan Swift, eds. Herbert Davis et al., 16 vols., Oxford, 1939–68.

The Correspondence of Jonathan Swift, ed. Harold Williams, rev. David Woolley, 5 vols., Oxford, 1963–72.

Jonathan Swift: The Complete Poems, ed. Pat Rogers, Middlesex, 1983.

Articles and Pamphlets

Andrews, J.H., "New Light on Three Eighteenth-Century Cartographers: Herman Moll, Thomas Moland and Henry Pratt" in *Bulletin of the Irish Georgian Society*, Vol. XXXV, 1992–3.

"Road Planning in Ireland before the Railway Age", *Irish Geography*, 5, No. 1, 1964.

Irish Maps, Irish Heritage Series, No. 18, Dublin, 1978.

Ball, F. Erlington, "An Episode in Swift's Southern Journey", *The Correspondence of Jonathan Swift D.D.*, ed. F.E. Ball, 6 vols., London, 1914, Vol. V, Appendix XVI.

"Swift Relics", *Correspondence*, Vol. VI, Appendix XII.

Bensly, Edward, "Swift's Welsh Travels", *N&Q*, 146, 29. 3. 1924.

Bracher, Frederick, "The Maps in Gulliver's Travels", *Huntington Library Quarterly*, 8, 1944–45.

Brooke, R.S., "A Pilgrimage to Quilca", *Dublin University Magazine*, 40, 1852.

Butler, T.R., Fitzwalter "Dean Swift and the Butlers", *Journal of the Butler Society*, Vol. 1, 1970–71.

Carpenter, Andrew, *The Irish Perspective of Jonathan Swift*, Wuppertal, 1978.

Carpenter, Andrew and Harrison, Alan, "Swift's 'O'Rourke's Feast' and Sheridan's 'Letter': Early Transcripts by Anthony Raymond", *Proceedings of the First Münster Symposium on Jonathan Swift*, eds. Hermann J. Real and Heinz J. Vienken, München, 1985.

"Swift, Raymond, and a Legacy", *Swift Studies*, 1986.

Case, Arthur E., "The Geography and Chronology of Gulliver's Travels", *Four Essays on Gulliver's Travels*, Princeton, 1945.

Churchill, R. C., "An Atlas of Fictional Geography", *Review of English Literature*, Vol. 7, 1966.

Corkery, Daniel, "Ourselves and Dean Swift", *Studies*, 23, 1934.

Cullen, Sara, "In the Sheridan Country", *Drumlin: Journal of Cavan, Leitrim and Monaghan*, 1, 1978.

Daly, Gerald, "George Semple's Charts of Dublin Bay, 1762", *Proceedings of the Royal Irish Academy*, Vol. 93, C, No. 3, 1993.

DePorte, Michael, "Swift's Horses of Instruction", *Reading Swift: Papers from the Second Münster Symposium on Jonathan Swift*, eds. Richard Rodino and Hermann J. Real, Munich, 1993.

Ehrenpreis, Irvin, "Swift's Voyages", *Modern Language Notes*, Vol. LXV, April, 1950.

Fagan, Patrick, "The Population of Dublin in the Eighteenth Century", *Eighteenth-Century Ireland*, 6, 1991.

Falkiner, Frederick, "Of the Portraits, Busts and Engravings of Swift and their Artists", *The Prose Works of Jonathan Swift, D.D.*, ed. Temple Scott, 12 vols., London, 1908, Vol. XII.

Hone, J.M., "Ireland and Swift", *Dublin Magazine*, 8, 1933.

Jackson, Robert Wyse, "Dean Swift's Tour of Munster", *Dublin Magazine*, 18, 1943.

Jackson, Victor, *St. Patrick's Cathedral, Dublin*, The Irish Heritage Series, No. 9, Dublin, 1976.

Jarrell, Mackie L., "'Jack and the Dane': Swift traditions in Ireland", *Fair Liberty Was All His Cry*, ed. A.N. Jeffares, Dublin, 1967.

Jeffares, A.N., "Place, Space and Personality and the Irish Writer", *Place, Personality and the Irish Writer*, ed. Andrew Carpenter, Gerrards Cross, 1977.

LeFanu, William R. "A Small Swift Archive", *Swift Studies*, 1986.

Lein, Clayton, "Jonathan Swift and the Population of Ireland", *Eighteenth Century Studies*, 8, 1974–75.

McCarvill, Eileen, "Jonathan Swift, Aodh Buí Mac Cruitín, and Contemporary Thomond Scholars", *North Munster Antiquarian Journal*, Vol. II, 1968.

McMinn, Joseph, "Jonathan's Travels – Swift's Sense of Ireland", *Swift Studies*, No. 7, 1992.

Mangan, Henry, "Portraits of Stella and Vanessa", *Journal to Stella*, ed. Harold Williams, 2 vols., Oxford, 1974, repr. 1986, Vol. II.

Moore, John Robert, "The Geography of Gulliver's Travels", *Journal of English and Germanic Philology*, 40, 1941.

Rankin, Helen, *A Short History of the Parish of Kilroot*, Belfast, 1982.

Reynolds, James, "Jonathan Swift – Vicar of Laracor", *Ríocht na Midhe: Records of the Meath Archaeological and Historical Society*, 4, 1967.

Ross, Ian Campbell, *Swift's Ireland*, The Irish Heritage Series, No. 39, Dublin, 1983.

Sherbo, Arthur, "Swift and Travel Literature", *Modern Language Studies*, 9, No. 3, 1979.

Simms, J. G., "Swift and County Armagh", *Seanchas Ard Mhacha*, Vol. 6, No. 1, 1971.

Torchiana, Donald, "Jonathan Swift, the Irish, and the Yahoos: The Case Reconsidered", *Philological Quarterly*, 54, 1975.

Ward, Isaac W., "The Black Family", *Ulster Journal of Archaeology*, Vol. VIII, 1902.

Williams, Harold, "Swift's Travels in Ireland 1714–35", *Correspondence*, Vol. V, Appendix XXXIII.

Wilson, T. G., "The Iconography of Swift", *Journal of the Royal College of Surgeons of Edinburgh*, 13, 1968.

"Pooley's Portrait of Swift", *Dublin Magazine*, 8, 1969.

Woolley, David, "Miscellanea in Two Parts: I. An Autograph, II. A Portrait", *Swift Studies*, No. 8, 1993.

"The Stemma of Gulliver's Travels: A First Note", *Swift Studies*, 1986.

Woolley, James, "Thomas Sheridan and Swift", *Studies in Eighteenth-Century Culture*, Vol. 9, 1980.

Books

Aalen, F.H. and Whelan, Kevin, (eds) *Dublin City and County: Prehistory to Present*, Dublin, 1992.

Andrews, J.H., *Plantation Acres*, Belfast, 1985.

Bence-Jones, Mark, *A Guide to Irish Country Houses*, rev. ed. London, 1988.
Brooke, Peter, *Ulster Presbyterianism*, Dublin, 1987.
Brownell, Morris R., *Alexander Pope and the Arts of Georgian England*, Oxford, 1978.
Butler, Patricia, *Three Hundred Years of Irish Watercolours and Drawings*, London, 1990.
Cahill, Susan and Thomas, *A Literary Guide to Ireland*, Dublin, 1979.
Cavan Historical Society, *Portrait of a Parish: A History of the Parish of Mullagh*, Cavan, 1988.
Craig, Maurice, *Dublin 1660–1800*, London, 1990.
The Architecture of Ireland from the Earliest Times to 1880, Dublin and London, 1982.
Cullen, Louis, *Merchants, Ships and Trade 1660–1830*, Dublin, 1971.
Day, Angélique, *Letters from Georgian Ireland: The Correspondence of Mary Delany*, Belfast, 1991.
Ehrenpreis, Irvin, *Swift: The Man, His Works and the Age*, 3 vols., London, 1962–83.
Elmes, Rosalind, *Catalogue of Irish Topographical Prints and Original Drawings*, revised and enlarged by Michael Hewson, Dublin, 1975.
Fabricant, Carole, *Swift's Landscape*, Baltimore and London, 1982.
Fagan, Patrick, *The Second City*, Dublin, 1986.
Ferguson, Oliver, W. *Jonathan Swift and Ireland*, Urbana, Illinois, 1962.
Foster, R.F. (ed.), *The Oxford Illustrated History of Ireland*, Oxford, 1989.
Galloway, Peter, *The Cathedrals of Ireland*, Belfast, 1992.
Gilligan. H.A., *A History of the Port of Dublin*, Dublin, 1988.
Glin, Knight of, Griffin, David, and Robinson, Nicholas, *Vanishing Country Houses of Ireland*, Dublin, 1989.
Godfrey, Ernest, *The Lindesays of Loughry, County Tyrone*, London, 1949.
Goldberg, Gerald, *Jonathan Swift and Contemporary Cork*, Cork, 1967.
Graby, John and O'Connor, Deirdre (eds), *Dublin Architecture Guide*, London, 1993.
Graham, Brian and Proudfoot, L.J. (eds), *The Historical Geography of Ireland*, London 1993.
Gwynn, Stephen, *The Life and Friendships of Dean Swift*, London, 1933.
Hadfield, Andrew and McVeagh, John (eds), *Strangers to that Land*, Gerrards Cross, 1994.
Harrington, John, *The English Traveller in Ireland*, Dublin, 1991.
Harrison, Alan, *Ag Cruinniú Meala*, Dublin, 1988.

Ireland, John DeCourcy, *Ireland and the Irish in Maritime History*, Dublin, 1986.

Johnston, Denis, *In Search of Swift*, Dublin, 1959.

Killanin, Lord and Duignan, Michael (eds), *The Shell Guide to Ireland*, revised by Peter Harbison, Dublin, 1989.

Landa, Louis, *Swift and the Church of Ireland*, Oxford, 1965.

McCaughan, Michael and Appleby, John (eds), *The Irish Sea: Aspects of Maritime History*, Belfast, 1989.

McSkimin, Samuel, *The History and Antiquities of the County of the Town of Carrickfergus*, third edition, Belfast, 1829.

Maxwell, Constantia, *Dublin under the Georges, 1714–1830*, Dublin, 1946.

The Stranger in Ireland, London, 1954.

Moody, T.W. and Vaughan, W.E. (eds), *A New History of Ireland*, Vol. IV: *Eighteenth Century Ireland 1691–1800*, Oxford, 1986.

Neely, W.G., *Kilkenny: An Urban History, 1391–1843*, Belfast, 1989.

Nowlan, K.B. (ed.), *Travel and Transport in Ireland*, Dublin, 1973.

Ó hÓgáin, Dáithí, *The Hero in Irish Folk History*, Dublin, 1985.

Passman, Dirk F., *Full of Improbable Lies: Gulliver's Travels und die Reiseliteratur vor 1726*, Frankfurt/M., New York, 1987.

Perceval-Maxwell, M., *The Scottish Migration to Ulster in the Reign of James I*, London, 1973.

Pilkington, Letitia, *Memoirs, 1712–1750*, Introduction by Iris Barry, London, 1928.

Piper, David, *Catalogue of the Seventeenth Century Portraits in the National Portrait Gallery, 1625–1714*, Cambridge, 1963.

Sheridan, Thomas, *The Life of Dr Swift*, London, 1784.

Somerville-Large, Peter, *Dublin: The First Thousand Years*, Belfast, 1988.

Strickland, W. G., *A Dictionary of Irish Artists*, 2 Vols, Shannon, 1969

Thompson, Paul and Dorothy (eds), *The Account Books of Jonathan Swift*, London and Newark, 1984.

A Jonathan Swift Daybook, unpublished manuscript in Ehrenpreis Center, Wilhelms-Westfälische Universität, Münster, Germany.

Tinniswood, Adrian, *A History of Country House Visiting*, Oxford, 1989.

Trevor, William, *A Writer's Ireland: Landscape in Literature*, London, 1984.

Watson, Edward, *The Royal Mail to Ireland*, London, 1917.

Wilde, William, *The Closing Years of Dean Swift's Life*, second edition, Dublin, 1849.

Williams, Harold, *Dean Swift's Library*, Cambridge, 1932.
Wilson, William, *The Post-Chaise Companion: or, Traveller's Directory through Ireland*, London and Dublin, 1784.
Woolley, James (ed.), *The Intelligencer*, Oxford, 1992.

Index

Page numbers in italics refer to illustrations. For Swift's writings, *see under* Swift, **Poetical Works**, and **Prose Works**.

Acheson, Sir Arthur and Lady, 119–32, 139
Aeolus, 114
Agher, Co. Meath 32
Aix-la-Chapelle, 68
Anglesey, Wales, 111
Anglicanism, 24, 29, 36, 38, 39, 87
Anne, Queen, 37
Antrim, County, 19, 21–31, 35, 39, *121*
Arbuthnot, Dr John, 140
Ardee, Co. Louth, 90
Ardsallagh, Co. Meath, 58, 67
Armagh, cathedral, *123*
  city, 66
  County, 66, 67, 76, 89, 90, 119–32, *121*, 135, 141
Arrowland, Co. Kildare, 58
Ashe, Dillon, 44
Ashe, St George, 44
Athlone, Co. Westmeath, 61
Athy, Co. Kildare, 58

Baldoyle, Co. Dublin, 131, 139
Ballinasloe, Co. Galway, 82
Ballinteggart House, Co. Armagh, *128*
Ballynure, Co. Antrim, 26, 28, 31
Baltimore, Co. Cork, 79
Bandon, Co. Cork, 78
Bangor, Wales, 106, 111
Barber, John, 147
Barber, Mary, 138
Beaumont, Joe, 42, 46
Bedell, Bishop William, 92
Belcamp, Raheny, Co. Dublin, 67, *see under* Grattan family
Belfast, Co. Antrim, 24, 26, 28, 29, 66
Belfast Lough, *27*
Bell, Peter, *113*
Belvedere, Earl of, 59
Berkeley, Earl of, 32, 33
Bert, Co. Kildare, 58
Bindon, Francis, 139, *see also* Swift, portraits of
Blachford, Rev. John, 140
Blamount, Co. Armagh, *128*
Bolingbroke, Viscount, 46
"Bolingbroke", Swift's horse, 65
Bolton, Dr John, 33
Bolton, Rev. Theophilus, 76, 82, 84, 141, 142
Boyne, river, 24, 29, 41
Brackdenstown, Co. Dublin, 96
Brandreth, Rev. John, 135
Brooking, Charles, *52*, *53*
Bryce, Rev. Edward, 26
Buck, Samuel and Nathaniel, *106*
Bunratty Castle, Co. Clare, 82

Burgh, Thomas, 51
Burnet, Thomas, *18*

Capel, Lord, 24
Carlingford Lough, 115
Carlisle, 106
Carnmoney, Co. Antrim, 29
Carrickfergus, Co. Antrim, 24, 27, 29
Carteret, Lord Lieutenant, 94, 97, 99, 101
Cashel, Co. Tipperary, 77, 141, *143*
Cassel (Castle), Richard, 53, 59
Castle Rackrent, 93
Castletown House, Co. Kildare, 53–4, *55*
Castletownshend, Co. Cork, 79
Catholic Confederation, 41
Cavan, County, 84, 89–104, 143–5, 144–5
Cave Hill, Co. Antrim, 24, *25*
Celbridge, Co. Kildare, 53, 57, 62–3, 84, 89
Celbridge Abbey, Co. Kildare, 54, 63, 64, *64*
Charlie, Bonnie Prince, 39
Chester, 46, 106–7, *107*, 110, *113*
Chetwode, Knightley, 55–9, 74, 76, 90, 96, 116–17
Clare, County, 82
Clogher, Co. Tyrone, 44, 66
Clonakilty, Co. Cork, 78
Cloncurry, Co. Kildare, 61
Cloney, Co. Kildare, 58
Clonfert, Co. Galway, 76, 82–4, *83*
Clonwarrir, Co. Kildare, 58
Coleraine, Co. Derry, 140
Connaught, 76
Connolly, William, 54
Cook, Thomas, *100*
Conway, Wales, 107, 111
Cope, Robert, 67, 76, 89, 90, 92
Cork, city 78
  County, 74, 77, 78, 79, *79*, 80, 146
Corkery, Daniel, 39
Counties of Ireland, *see under* individual names
Coventry, 107
Cox, Sir Richard, 78
Cox, Roger, 42
Cromwell, 19, 21, 41, 106
Cross Keys, Co. Cavan, 144
Cumberland, 106

Daingean, Co. Offaly, 56
Dawson, Joshua, 52
Dee, river, 106
de Lacy, Hugh, 41

Delany, Patrick, 60, 65, 71, 102, 138
de Morville, Comte, 110
Denham, John, 126
Derry, city, 51
  County, 33, 51, 140
  Deanery of, 33
Derry Society, The, 141
Dicksee, Margaret, *23*
Dingley, Rebecca, 22, 43, 77, 84, 92–3, 98, 104
Dissenters, 26, 29, 30, 35, 38
Dobbs, Richard, 26–7
Donegal, County, 54
Dopping, Rev. Samuel, 68
Dorset, Duke of, 135, 143
Down, County, 24, 26, 66, 119, *120*
Drogheda, Co. Louth, 24, 66, 119
Drogheda, Earl of, 59
Dromoland Castle, Co. Clare, 82
Dromore, Co. Down, 28
Drumlack, Co. Armagh, 126
Dublin, city, *52*
  architecture, 51–4
  bay, 106
  Capel Street, 53, 91, 119
  Christchurch cathedral, 23, 51, 52
  College Green, 51
  Coombe, 21
  Corporation, 52, 102
  Custom House, 51, *138*
  Dame Street, *144*
  Dublin Castle, 21, 32, 100, *146*
  Essex Bridge, 53, *138*
  Essex Street, 51
  Hoey's Court, 21
  King's Inns, 21
  Leinster House, 53
  Liberties, 84
  Liffey, river, 51, 54, 64, *87*, 91, 106, *138*
  Ormonde Quay, 85
  Oxmanstown Green, 52
  Parkgate, 52
  Parliament House, 54, 55, 143, *144*
  Phoenix Park, 52, 84
  population, 51
  Royal Barracks, 52
  Royal Hospital, Kilmainham, 51, *53*, 84
  St Andrew's Round Church, 145
  St Bridget Street, 21
  St Mary's Parish, 53
  St Michan's Parish, 53
  St Patrick's cathedral, 21, 22, 33, 41, 47, 48, 51, *70*, 91, 96, 101, 149
  St Patrick's hospital, 142
  St Patrick Street, 21

157

St Stephen's Green, 52
St Werburgh, 21
Skinner's Row, 52
Swift's attitude to, 67, 125, 137–8, 140, 143
Swift's friends in, 65, 138–9
Tholsel, 52
Trinity College, 22, 45, 51, 52, 145
Turnstile Alley, 54, 62
Dublin, County, 16, 17, 24, 28, 43, 44, 51–73, *56*, 74, 84, 91, 96, 98, 104, 110, 115, 119, 121, 131, 133, 137–140, 143
Dublin Intelligencer, 129
Dunboyne, Co. Meath, 84
Dundalk, Co. Louth, 24, 90, 115, 119
Dungannon, Co. Tyrone, 66
Dunkin, William, 80
Dunlavin, Co. Wicklow, 33
Dunmanway, Co. Cork, 78
Dunshaughlin, Co. Meath, 144
Dunstable, 107

Edgeworth, Maria, 93
Effernock, Co. Meath, 49
Ehrenpreis, Irvin, 11, 40
Ennis, Co. Clare, 82
Enniskillen, Co. Fermanagh, 66
Erick, Abigail, *see under* Swift, family

Fabricant, Carole, 11
Farran, George, *67*
Farren, Thomas, 146
Faulkner, George, *45*, 104, 137, 142
Fennor, Co. Tipperary, 141
Ferguson, O.W., 11
Fermanagh, County, 66, 90
Finglas, Co. Dublin, 44, 65, 103
First Fruits, 37, 46, 49
Fisher, Jonathan, *85*, *87*
Fog's Weekly Journal, 126
Foot, Michael, 9–10
Foras Feasa ar Éirinn, 78
Ford, Charles, 44, 58, 64, 68, 69–70, 73, 77, 84–6, 87, 90, 95, 102–3, 138–9

Galway, County, 51, 59, 74, 77, 82–3, 136
Gaulstown, Co. Westmeath, 59–61, *60*, 62, 92, *see also* Rochfort family
Gay, John, 44, 130
George I, King, 110, *138*
George II, King, 110
Glasnevin, Co. Dublin, 138
Godolphin, Lord, 37
Goodrich, Herefordshire, 109
Gosford, Viscount, 131
Gosford Castle, 132, *132*
GPA-Bolton Library, Cashel, Co. Tipperary, 143
Grafton, Duke of, 94
Grattan, family, 65, 85, 96, 101, 139, 147
Grose, Francis, *81*, *142*

Hamilton's Bawn, Co. Armagh, 121
Hanover, 110
Harding, John, 96, 129
Harding, Sarah, 129
Harley, Edward, *see* Oxford, Earl of
Hart Hall, 22
Helsham, Dr Richard, 138
Hibernia Anglicana, 78, *see* Cox, Richard
Hiberniae Delineatio, *see under* Petty, William
Holyhead, Wales, 106, *106*, 107, 110–118
Howth, Co. Dublin, 139, *139*, 140
Hussey, Philip, *63*

Innsbruck, 136
Irish Sea, *see under* Swift, travels

Jackson, Rev. Dan, 61, 65
Jackson, Rev. John, 65
James II, King, 22, 24
Jenny, Dr Henry, 76
Jervas, Charles, 61, *69*
Johnson, Esther, "Stella", 22, *23*, 43, 45, *45*, 46, 47, 54, 77, 84–5, 92–3, 98, 104, 110, 112–18, *117*
Jonathan Swift Art Gallery, Kilroot, Co. Antrim, 31
Jonson, Ben, 126

Keating, Geoffrey, 78
Kells, Co. Meath, 91, 98, 144
Kerry, County, 19, 80–1
Kilberry, Co. Kildare, 58
Kilcolman, Co. Kildare, 58
Kilcoole, Co. Wicklow, 140
Kildare, County, 53, 58, 61, 62, 77
Kildare, Earls of, 53
Kilkenny, County, 21, 77, 135, 141
Kilkenny College, 21
Killarney, Co. Kerry, 80
Kilroot, Co. Antrim, 21–31, *30*, 32, 33, 42, 43
King, Archbishop William, 42, 43, 61, 143–4
King's County, *see under* Offaly, County
Kinsale, Co. Cork, 78, 99
Knightsbrook, John, 33
Knightsbrook, river, 41
Knightsbrook Gate, Co. Meath, 43
Knocktopher, Co. Kilkenny, 135

Lambert, Rev. Ralph, 66
Langford, Sir Arthur, 33, 43
Laois, County, 55–7, 92
Laracor, Co. Meath, 32–50, *50*, 55, 66, 67
Latham, James, *117*
Leicester, 21, 22, 108
Leinster, *34*
Leixlip, Co. Kildare, 61, 84, *85*, *87*
Limerick, city, 82
County, 77, 80

Lindsay, Robert, 89
Lisburn, Co. Antrim, 24, 66
London, 30, 34, 38, 40, 44, 46, 51, 56, 104, 107, 108, 109, 110, 113–4, 115, 126, 127, 129, 133, 137, 140, 146, 147
Lough Derg, 82
Lough Ennell, 59, *60*
Lough Erne, 90
Lough Neagh, 90
Lough Ramor, 91, *94*
Loughbrickland, Co. Down, 29
Loughgall, Co. Armagh, 67, 89–90, *91*
Louth, County, 24, 90, 115, 119
Lucan, Co. Dublin, *87*
Ludlow, Peter, 58, 67

McAulay, Alexander, 102
McFadden, Elizabeth, 91, *see also* Sheridan, Thomas
Mac Gauran, Hugh, 71
Magherafelt, Co. Derry, 67
Magheralin, Co. Down, 66, 67
maps, *16*, 17, *27*, *34*, *49*, *56*, *75*, *79*, *101*, 112, *113*, *120*, *see also* Moll, Herman, *and* Petty, William
Markethill, Co. Armagh, 119–32, *128*
Markievicz, Constance, *67*
Marsh, Narcissus, 22, 23
Marsh's Library, 51
Martry, Co. Meath, *56*, 76
Maryborough (Portlaoise), 77
Maynooth, Co. Kildare, 84
Meath, County, 19, 58, 76, 84, 143, 144
Midleton, Co. Cork, 146
Moll, Herman, *34*, *120*, *134*
Molesworth, Robert, 59, 96
Molyneux, William, 27
Monaghan, County, 90
Moor Park, Surrey, 22, 28, 29, 30–1, 32, 36
Moore, Lady Betty, 59
Moreton, William, 23
Motte, Benjamin, 108, 109
Muckross Abbey, Co. Kerry, 81, *81*, 82
Mullaghbrack, Co. Armagh, 76
Mullingar, Co. Westmeath, 119
Munster, 74–88, *75*
Myross, Co. Cork, 78, 79

"Naboth's Vineyard", 96, 98
Navan, Co. Meath, 44, 56, 66
Newry, Co. Down, 24, 66, 90, 119
Nixon, John, *24*

Ó Carolan, Turlough, 71
O'Neill, Hugh, 79
Ó Rathaille, Aogán, 80–2
Offaly, County, 56, 61, 84
Oldcourt, Co. Kildare, 58
Ormonde, Duke of, 21, 52
Orrery, Lord, 42, 138, 142, 146
Oxford, Earl of, 46, 143
Oxford, University, 22, 29

Pale, the, 24, 33, 66
Parkgate, 106, 110, *113*
Parnell, Rev. Thomas, 44, *45*
Parsivol, Isaiah, 42
Pearce, Edward Lovett, 54, 143, 145
Penmaenmawr, Wales, 111
Petty, William, 18, *34, 49, 56, 79, 101*
Phillipstown (Daingean), Co. Offaly, 56
Pilkington, Laetitia, 138
Place, Francis, *107*
Pope, Alexander, 44, 72–3, 108, 110, *111*, 125, 133, 137
Portadown, Co. Armagh, 126
Portarlington, Co. Laois, 55
Portlaoise, Co. Laois, 77
Portumna, Co. Galway, 82
Powerscourt, Co. Wicklow, 134
presbyterianism, Ulster, 24, 25, 26, 27, 36, 38, 39, 123–4, 137
Prusselstown, Co. Kildare, 58
Ptolemy, 112

Queen's County, *see under* Laois, County
Quilca, Co. Cavan, 84, 89–104

Rantavan, Co. Cavan, 91
Rathbeggan, Co. Meath, 33
Ratoath, Co. Meath, 143
Raymond, Rev. Anthony, 42, 43, 45
Reformation, the, 26
Restoration, the, 21
Revolution, Glorious, 24, 26
Richardson, William, 140
Ridland, Wales, 111
Rincurran, Co. Cork, 99
Ringsend, Co. Dublin, 106
Robinson, William, 51
Rochfort family, 59, 61, 77, 84, 119, *see also* Gaulstown
Rochfortbridge, Co. Westmeath, 59
Ross Carbery, Co. Cork, 78, 80
Royal School, Cavan, 143
Russelstown, Co. Kildare, 58
Rysbrack, Peter, *111*

St Albans, 107
St Brendan, 83
St Colman, 26, 31
St John the Baptist cathedral, Cashel, Co. Tipperary, 143
St John of God Brothers, *64*
St Patrick's cathedral, *see under* Dublin, city
Sandby, Paul, *40*
Santry, Co. Dublin, 60, 65
Savage, Anne, 119
Savage, Phillip, 119
Scotland, 26, 35, 38, 144
Scriblerus Society, 44
Semple, George, *70*
Shannon, river, 82, 84
Shanrahan, Co. Kildare, 58
Sheridan, Denis, 92

Sheridan, Richard Brinsley, 91
Sheridan, Thomas, friend of Swift, 60, 74, 84, 89, 90, 91, 92, 93, 97, 99, *100*, 101, 103, 121, 123, 138, 143–5
Sheridan, Thomas, biographer, 91
Sixmilebridge, Co. Clare, 82
Skibbereen, Co. Cork, 78
Sliabh Luachra, Co. Kerry, 80
Slieve Aughty, Co. Clare, 82
Sobieski, Clementina, 136
Somerville, Edith and Ross, Martin, 79
Somerville, Rev. Phillip, 79
Spenser, Edmund, 78
Stannard, Eaton, 146
Stearne, Rev. John, 41, 42, 43, 66, 89
"Stella", *see under* Johnson, Esther
Stopford, James, 104
Story, George, *27*
Swift, Jane, sister of Jonathan, 21
Swift, Godwin, uncle of Jonathan, 21, 77
Swift, Jonathan, father of Jonathan, 21
Swift, Jonathan (1667–1745)
  career in England, 30, 46–7
  childhood, 21–2, 77, 105–6
  Church of Ireland, 15, 19, 23, 26, 28, 29, 33, 37, 39, 41, 47, 49–50, 54, 58, 65, 123–4, 145
  education, 21–2
  family, 21, 38, 77, 109–10
  Freeman, of Cork, 146, of Dublin, 102
  personality, 11, 20
  portraits, illustrations, of *18, 23*, 61, *69*, 139, *148*
  travels: accidents, 61, 79–80, 112; benefits of, reasons for, 17, 24, 55, 61, 74, 76–7, 89, 96, 105; card-games, 43, 44, 122; civilisation, sense of, 15, 58, 63, 72, 89, 92, 103, 108–9, 121, 123, 134–5; coach-travel, 56, 60, 141; duration, timing of, 17, 67, 75, 121, 125, 134; distances covered, 19, 44, 55, 57, 66, 74, 84, 88, 90, 105, 107, 119; England, sense of, 35, 36, 38, 72–3, 95, 97, 104; ferry-travel, 65, 111, *134*; folklore, 74, 78, 80–2; food, 82, 144–5; gardening and building, love of, 33, 39, 40, 41–2, 44, 57–8, 60, 96, 98, 120–2, 126–8, 141; Gaelic Ireland, 39, 42, 71, 78–9, 82, 92, 136–7; health, 15, 19, 61–2, 64, 68–9, 77, 93, 95, 98, 116–17, 125, 140, 141, 143; horses, 17, *18*, 44, 60, 65, 68, 96, 97, 111, 112, 143; imagination, 15, 149; Ireland, sense of, 19, 35, 36, 39, 43, 48, 54, 70–1, 72–3, 86, 104, 105, 116, 128–9, 135–6; landlords, 72; landscape, views on, 11, 12, 17, 57, 58, 70, 84, 89–90, 100, 104, 112, 116, 118, 124, 135; language, 15,

80; literary strategies, 30, 34–5, 36, 46, 134; memory, 29; money, 36, 43, 48–9, 58, 68, 96, 106, 107, 127, 139–40; Nature, 116; pastoral, 47–8, 80, 93; placenames, 26, 41, 58, 86, 91; places visited, *16*, *see also under individual counties*; Protestant Ireland, 71–2, 78, 86, 95, 102, 126; reading, 89; romanticism, 12, 78; roads, 17, 77, 132, 140, 141; servants, 19, 65, 68, 79–80, 93, 110–15; sea-travel, 28, 32, 33, 36, 37, *37*, 105–118, 138; tourist, 17.

Poetical Works
The Blessings of a Country Life, 98
Cadenus and Vanessa, 54
Carberiae Rupes, 80
A Character, Panegyric, and Description of the Legion Club, 145–6
The Dean's Reasons for not Building at Drapier's Hill, 127–8
The Description of an Irish Feast, 70–1
Drapier's Hill, 126–7
Holyhead, 25 September, 1727, 115–16
My Lady's Lamentation, 122
On the Little House by the Churchyard at Castleknock, 44–6
Ode to the King, 24–5
A Panegyric on the Dean, 130–1
The Part of a Summer, 62
The Plagues of a Country Life, 98–9
To Quilca, 103
Stella at Woodpark, 84–5
Verses on the Death of Dr Swift, 147

Prose Works
The Blunders, Deficiencies, Distresses, and Misfortunes of Quilca, 93
A Complete Collection of Genteel and Ingenious Conversation, 134
Directions to Servants, 134
The Drapier's Letters, 94–7, 99–102, 129
Fraud Detected: Or, The Hibernian Patriot, 104
Gulliver's Travels, 11, 15, 73, 86–8, 102–3, 104, 106, 108, *108*, 109, *109*
Holyhead Journal, 112–16
The Intelligencer, 123–5
Journal to Stella, 46–7
A Letter from a Member of the House of Commons in Ireland to a Member of the House of Commons in England Concerning the Sacramental Test, 38
A Letter to a Very Young Lady, on her Marriage, 62
A Modest Proposal, 128–9
A Proposal for the Universal Use of Irish Manufacture, 72
A Short View of the State of Ireland, 124–5
The Story of the Injured Lady, 35, 36–7
A Tale of a Tub, 30, 32, 34

Works, George Faulkner, 142
Swifte's Heath, Co. Kilkenny, 77
Switzerland, 104
Swords, Co. Dublin, 96

Tandragee, Co. Armagh, 121
Temple, John, 36
Temple, Sir William, 22, 23, 32, 36, 43
Templecorran, Co. Antrim, 26
Test Act, Sacramental, 38, 137
Thames, river, 108
Tipperary, County, 21, 27, 141, 142–3
Torbay, 22
Tories, 46
Towcester, 107
Towers, Rev. John, 134
Townshend, Colonel Bryan, 79
Trim, Co. Meath, 40–1, *40*, 42, 43, 55, 57, 58, 66–7, 77
Trinity College Dublin, *see under* Dublin, city
Tudor, Joseph, *138*, *144*, *146*
Tullygorey, Co. Kildare, 58
Twickenham, 108, 109, 110, *111*

Tyrellstown, Co. Kildare, 58
Tyrone, County, 44, *49*, 66, 79, 89

Ulster, plantation of, 26, 79
  map of, 101

Van Der Hagen, Johann, *37*
Van Homrigh, Esther, "Vanessa", 47–8, 54, 56–7, 60, 62, *63*, 64, *64*, 74–5, 76, 89, 90
Van Homrigh, Mary, "Molkin", *63*, 64
Versailles, 110
Virgil, 80
Virginia, Co. Cavan, 91, *94*, 143
Voltaire, 110

Wales, 105, 106, 110–18
Walpole, Horace, 110
Walsh, Rev. John, 141
Walls, Rev. Thomas, 57, 65
Warburton, Thomas, 40, 45, 67
Ware, Sir James, *70*, *123*
Waring, Jane, "Varina", 28, 41, 66

Waringstown, Co. Down, 28, 66
Watt, Swift's servant, 110–15
Wesley, Garrett, 33, 43
Westmeath, County, 59, 61, 84, 119
Wheatley, Francis, *139*
Wheldon, John, 114–15
Whigs, 37, 46, 47, 59
Whitchurch, 107
Whitehaven, 105–6
Whiteway, Mrs, 144–5, 147
Wicklow, County, 33, 112, 134, 140
William of Orange, King, 19, 22, 24, 25, 27, 29, 39
Winder, Rev. John, 28–9
Windsor, 62–3, 109
Wogan, Charles, 136–7
Wood, William, 94
Wood Park, Co. Meath, 44
Woodbrooke, Co. Laois, 55–7, 92
"Woodlands", Raheny, Co. Dublin, 65
Worrall, John, 101

Yeats, W.B., 149
Young, Arthur, 131–2